# Better Dog Behavior

A KENNEL CLUB BOOK™

## IN APPRECIATION

Books are the products of many minds, hands and hearts all working together to make it happen. This book is a perfect example of that.

The photos were taken by Beverly Walter, an accomplished and prize-winning photographer, who spends hours researching her subjects and following them around to catch just the right message in each picture. Thank you, Bev; it has been my privilege to work with you.

Editor Andrew DePrisco, himself a book author of note, makes a great guide for writers trying to convey messages in print. He's eagle-eyed, understanding and patient, and a pro at mastering the use of the written word. He makes my job look better than I ever thought it could!

As the author, I have used my mind, hands and heart to address and solve the many behavior problems of our canine companions. Each dog I've lived with and each dog I've trained has added to my store of knowledge and experience, from which I derive the help I offer herein. It has been a special treat for me to compile this guide and present it to dog owners everywhere. Dogs have made my life an exceptional wonder—I hope your dog makes your life wonderful, too.

**Photography by Beverly Walter**
with additional photos by
Mary Bloom, Paulette Braun, Bernd Brinkmann,
Isabelle Français, Carol Ann Johnson, Nancy Liguori,
Antonio Phillipe, Alice Roche, Nikki Sussman,
Michael Trafford and Alice van Kempen.

**KENNEL CLUB BOOKS: BETTER DOG BEHAVIOR**
**ISBN: 1-59378-379-5**

**Copyright © 2004**
Kennel Club Books, Inc., 308 Main Street, Allenhurst, NJ 07711 USA
Cover Design Patented: US 6,435,559 B2 • Printed in South Korea

# Better Dog Behavior

## CORRECTING AND CURING BAD HABITS

◆

*By Charlotte Schwartz*

7 . . . . . . . . Foreword

9 . . . . . Introduction

## 13                  Aggression

A problem that can occur in dogs of any breed, aggression has different forms and causes. Learn about each type of aggression and remedial methods that owners can try at home.

## 24                  Barking

Some dogs have a lot to say! Learn the difference between instinctive, appropriate barking and excessive nuisance barking, and how to correct the latter.

## 34                  Carsickness

Acclimate your dog to riding in the car so that you can travel safely and happily together.

## 39                  Chasing

Learn about prey drive, hunting instinct and other factors that cause dogs to chase people, other animals, vehicles, etc., and how to discourage this potentially dangerous behavior.

## 43                  Chewing

Find out how to direct your dog's chewing needs and energies onto appropriate objects and discourage destructive chewing.

## 55                  Coprophagia

A canine habit considered one of the most disgusting by humans, stool eating is commonly seen in dogs and can be controlled with simple preventative measures.

## 56                  Digging

What dog doesn't love to get his paws dirty every once in a while? Whether your dog is a compulsive or recreational digger, learn how to keep digging from becoming destructive.

## 60            Fear of Thunder and Other Noises

If your dog fears certain sounds, the desensitization technique presented here is effective in acclimating him to the noises that usually make him run and hide.

# Contents

## House-training and Urine Marking 64

Study a proven crate-training method to teach your dog clean toileting habits and learn how to deal with territorial urine-marking behavior.

## Inappropriate Play Behavior 73

Direct your dog's playful exuberance into constructive activities and avoid those which foster aggressive, rough and otherwise undesirable tendencies.

## Jumping 78

Jumping to say hi, to look out a window, to clear a fence and more—dogs jump for many reasons and owners can train their dogs to control this behavior.

## Running Away 92

Teaching your dog to come reliably when called is the solution to preventing his running away from you and into danger.

## Separation Anxiety 98

Dogs live for companionship and can suffer without enough attention. Learn how to tailor your busy schedule to make your dog feel secure as part of the family pack.

## Shyness 109

Whether genetic or environmental, shyness can be eased with a method of gentle socialization and rehabilitation to replace your dog's fears with confidence.

## Stealing Food 120

Most dogs are perpetual "chow-hounds" and will find a way to get their paws on forbidden food unless taught otherwise. Learn how to stop a thief!

Index . . . . . . . . 126

**Shake hands with a well-mannered, well-trained delightful dog— *your* dog!**

# FOREWORD

From time to time, we've all heard dog owners complain about their dogs' bad habits—things like incessant barking, digging in the flower garden, jumping on people, stealing food from the table, being aggressive toward people or other dogs, running away, etc. There are probably as many behavior problems among dogs as there are among people, so it is no wonder that dog owners get frustrated when trying to deal with their dogs' undesirable behavior. This book will help you correct and cure these problems.

*"My dog is uncontrollable!"*

*"My dog drives me crazy with his constant barking."*

*"Every time I open my front door, the dog runs out and it takes me hours to catch him."*

*"I can't leave any food out on the counter because my dog jumps up and steals it."*

*"My dog chases the cat constantly."*

If you recognize any of these problems in your own dog or if you feel that you'd like to correct some other annoying habit that your dog displays, read on. This book addresses many problems exhibited by dogs. Some of these problems irritate or annoy people, while other types of behavior can be dangerous or threatening to the well-being of people or other pets.

Some of these problems and solutions are simple. Some are complex. If you are facing a behavior problem with your dog, this book will guide you through the steps necessary to correct the problem and restore the healthy relationship you expect to have with your canine partner. After all, your dog should be your companion, not your headache.

Dog aggression, chasing cars, jumping on furniture, stealing food from the table and destructive chewing are just some of the behaviors addressed in this book. But before we can attempt to change behaviors we don't want, we must understand the hows and whys of behavior problems. For example, why does one dog choose to chase cars and bicycles while another ignores them? Why does one dog lift his leg and urinate on his owner's favorite chair while another never has "accidents" in the house?

By having an understanding of exactly what causes problem behaviors and the knowledge of how to modify or alter them, we can save innumerable dogs from being turned over to animal shelters because their owners cannot cope with their beloved yet misbehaving pets. Sometimes the solution is simple, perhaps a matter of a slight change in the dog's environment, schedule or activities. In other cases, the cause and treatment of a behavior problem will require extensive work to correct or modify. Only in a very small number of cases will a behavior be impossible to change. In those cases, the owner needs to understand that, in all likelihood,

he was powerless to initiate a change in the dog.

Whatever your dog's problem, let this book help you as if it were a ranger guiding you through a forest of troubles and solutions. Read on and discover the positive methods that can alter your dog's behavior for life and give the two of you a renewed and rewarding relationship. Pay particular attention to the fact that, in most cases of problem-solving, negative reinforcement is neither necessary nor required. Only by positive measures recognizing and acknowledging the dog's desirable behaviors will the dog begin to understand what is and is not acceptable behavior.

**A polite posed quartet, sitting pretty and enjoying some fresh air.**

# INTRODUCTION

Exactly what is a dog behavior problem? A behavior problem to one owner may not be a behavior problem to another. Take jumping up on the owner, for instance. One owner may encourage his dog to jump up on him while the other owner tries to teach the dog not to jump up. The second owner reasons that if the dog is allowed to jump up on his owner, he'll jump up on other people as well. This is easily managed by teaching the dog not to jump up on anyone but the owner or other family members. It often surprises people to learn that dogs can comprehend the difference between family and guests. Dogs are surprisingly astute at figuring out who will allow jumping and who will not.

So, to get back to our question, what is a behavior problem? The answer is any behavior that the owner finds unacceptable and undesirable. It could be a relatively simple problem like the dog's habit of jumping up on people, or a more complicated behavior like destroying the owner's possessions when the dog is left alone. What it boils down to is that a problem is whatever your dog does that you don't appreciate and that you wish to either moderately alter or entirely eliminate.

It must be made abundantly clear that no book can cover and solve *all* problem behaviors found in dogs. The subject can cover a host of volumes, depending on how involved the problems are. There then can be a plethora of possible solutions, depending on the complexity of those involvements.

Let's take that jumping-up problem. Do you want to correct the dog for jumping up on people? How about jumping on forbidden furniture? Then there's the problem of fence and barrier jumping. Is that a behavior you'd like to stop because it's a nuisance for you to have to go fetch the dog from his roamings around the neighborhood? Furthermore, it's a serious matter of the dog's risk of being hit by a car and killed when he does escape the security of his own yard. You can see here that some behaviors have many aspects to be considered, while others, such as motion sickness, are less complicated. In this instance, the dog doesn't get sick anywhere else, just when he rides in the car. This problem, then,

Once a dog is comfortable in his surroundings and properly trained, his personality can really emerge.

is more easily addressed and corrected.

I have taken the most common problems that plague dog owners and compiled an alphabetical guide to these problems and possible solutions. These are problems with which I deal on a daily basis. The dogs involved range from St. Bernards to Shetland Sheepdogs to Chihuahuas, and everything in between! All breeds and mixed breeds can and do present behaviors that their owners find objectionable.

It may surprise you to know that a large portion of the causes of dog behavior problems are created by the owners. You see, a dog's behavior problem is frequently created by the dog's environment. A dog's relationship with his owners, his family members, is part of that environment. Therefore a problem may develop as a result of some action or response that the owner exhibits without even realizing the effect it has on the dog.

For example, the owner bends down to pet his puppy. The puppy squats down in front of the owner and loses bladder control, which makes him urinate at the owner's feet. The owner sees the puddle and reprimands the dog for wetting the floor. The puppy hears the disapproval in his master's voice and cowers away. Unfortunately, the puppy now believes that the owner's bending down in front of him will result in his being scolded,

so the puppy quickly learns to avoid his owner.

This behavior, in turn, infuriates the owner, who thinks that the puppy doesn't want to be with him. This causes him to become frustrated, so he yells even more at the poor puppy. This vicious cycle continues until the dog wets the

> ## OTHER CAUSES
> Stress can be a significant factor in creating problem behaviors in dogs. Disease, emotional trauma, inherited factors (genetic components), environmental conditions, learning experiences and even developmental factors can all cause or contribute to behavior problems. The dog's basic temperament, such as dominance or submissiveness, can also have some bearing on a behavior problem.

floor every time the owner comes near and the owner begins to dislike the puppy because he sees him as a dirty and disobedient dog.

In order to be successful at solving the problem and either altering or eliminating it, we must determine the relationship between the dog, his behavior and his environment. Therefore the relationship a dog has with his owner becomes a major element in changing the dog's problem behavior. Let's get started in exploring the various problems, along with their causes and possible solutions.

Children must be careful when dealing with dogs on the other side of a fence so that they do not tease the dog or otherwise encourage territorial behavior.

# AGGRESSION

There are two basic kinds of aggression in dogs: aggression toward humans and aggression toward other dogs or other animals. In both cases, the reasons for the aggressive behavior are as varied as the dogs themselves. For example, genetic aggression is caused by heredity and requires professional help. Lack of socialization with other dogs and with people when the dog was very young is often found to be a contributing factor to dog aggression. When the dog lacks proper early socialization, he fails to develop self-confidence. That, in

The brown dog takes a posture of defending his territory against the white dog's advances, even though a fence separates the two.

turn, creates shyness, which can lead to defensive and/or fear-biting behavior.

Topical aggression is caused by something in the dog's environment. Sometimes aggression is a result of circumstances in the dog's life that cause the dog's basic instincts to respond inappropriately. (This is sometimes referred to as learned behavior.) Say, for instance, the dog was abused by a man when he was a young puppy. The dog grows up believing that men are cruel, so, to protect himself, he becomes aggressive toward all men. Then, of course, there are always cases of aggression in

## A SERIOUS MATTER

Aggression in dogs is a serious matter. So serious, in fact, that there are books devoted only to the subject. There are seminars and educational courses given on dog aggression. There are dog trainers and animal behaviorists who specialize in the subject and veterinary scholars who spend their entire professional careers studying this type of behavior. In short, dog aggression is a major concern to those who deal with it on either a professional or personal level in their own home.

which the cause is never determined and the solution is uncertain at best.

Aggression is divided by many behaviorists into general classifications. Each classification suggests the cause of the aggression, which, in turn, helps to determine the route of corrective treatment. Territorial aggression occurs when a dog defends something such as his home, yard, toys, food and, in some cases, his owner. Predatory aggression includes chasing moving objects such as other animals, children, bicycles, cars, etc. Sexual aggression usually occurs between two males contending for mating privileges with a particular female. Maternal aggression occurs when a female has a litter of puppies and feels the need to protect them. There is even a classification known as irritable aggression. An example of this is a very old dog who does not want to be annoyed by enthusiastic, noisy children, so he growls whenever they come near as he rests. Likewise, some females in season become irritable and snappy during their periods of estrus. Finally, fearful aggression is a common condition seen during visits to the vet.

Generally territorial, sexual and irritable aggression are seen in dominant-type dogs, while fearful aggression is usually found in submissive ones. Whatever the target or cause of dog aggression, we must be concerned with its consequences to others. A bite is a bite, and excuses are unacceptable when it comes to dog bites. Some biting habits can be corrected, some cannot. Occasionally we see severe cases that can be corrected under the supervision of a behaviorist and a vet who prescribes drugs to lower the dog's level of aggression. Let's examine some types of aggression with which owners can deal themselves to correct the problem.

## TYPES OF AGGRESSION

### AGGRESSION TOWARD PEOPLE

First, let's look at aggression toward people. Sometimes a dog is afraid of people because he doesn't know them and feels threatened by them. Very likely, as a young puppy he wasn't exposed to other people in a variety of situations and environments. Or perhaps someone abused him and those negative experiences have taught him to avoid all people in order to protect himself.

Creating a happy, rewarding experience for the dog is what you, as the owner, need to do to turn things around. Always work with your dog on lead so you can maintain control at all times. Gradually expose the dog to only one or two people at a time, under quiet conditions.

Begin by having the dog sit next to you in the middle of a room. Never position yourself in a corner with the dog, as this will only reinforce the dog's fear of being trapped. A friend (who is unfamiliar to the dog and to whom you have provided some doggie treats) should casually approach the two of you without making any eye contact with the dog. The person should have a special treat, such as a piece of cooked chicken or beef, in his hand. As the person approaches, he should speak to you with a soft, happy voice, as if he were meeting an old friend, while ignoring the dog.

The person should stop in front of the two of you at a distance that the dog finds acceptable. If the person gets too close, the dog will probably get up. Thus you want the person to stop before the dog feels uncomfortable

and attempts to retreat. The person should have the treat in his hand and should keep his arm extended downward so the dog can see and smell the treat without having to look up.

As the dog reaches forward to investigate the treat in the person's hand, he may try to take it. The person should hold the treat in his open palm so the dog can easily get the food. As soon as the dog takes the treat, both of you (the owner and the friend) should praise the dog. The person then puts another treat in his hand, and you all repeat the process: the hand is held down in front of the person with open palm, the dog takes the treat, both people praise the dog.

Soon the dog begins to get the idea that having this new person around is pretty nice, because the person talks kindly and gives him

Under adult supervision, carefully approaching and with a treat in hand is the best way to make introductions between a child and dog.

## WITH CHILDREN

Maybe the person in question is a child, and the dog has never been exposed to children; therefore, he finds their erratic behavior and squealy voices unsettling. He warns them to stay away with growls and snarls. If the child doesn't heed the warning, the dog may bite. Or perhaps children have teased the dog in the past, so he's learned to distrust all little people. When he finds himself unable to avoid them, he may turn to biting.

treats. When the friend can approach you and your dog in various places and under various conditions (in your yard, on a footpath with other people walking nearby, in places where there are children and adults going about their business), then the dog is ready to be introduced to another stranger. By now the first person has become an old familiar friend to the dog, so it's time to bring in some new friendly faces. It is advisable to introduce the dog to the new stranger in the presence of the first person to whom you introduced the dog. This should take place in quiet surroundings, where the dog doesn't feel stressed. (Remember, change only one factor at a time so the dog will not become so stressed that he reacts inappropriately.)

As the dog becomes accustomed to having strangers approach him and you (his owner) in a friendly manner, he will begin to relax. As he does, he'll probably begin approaching his new "friends" on his own, simply because he anticipates a treat and the pleasant experience of meeting them. Little by little, the new friends will be able to reach down and offer a hand to the dog as a greeting. At first, people should pet him only on the side of his neck or head, or under his chin. People should never attempt to pet him on the top of the head, as this gesture may serve as a threatening behavior to him. Let the dog initiate the overtures of friendship. His friends need just to be there to encourage him when he shows a willingness to try.

### AGGRESSION TOWARD CHILDREN

Usually dogs that exhibit aggressive behavior toward children do so for one of two reasons. The first reason is that a child or children have agitated the dog in the past. Often a dog that spends time alone in a fenced yard will be teased by children outside the

TOP: Two dogs meet.
BOTTOM: The dog on the right is dominant while the dog on the left says with his body language, "OK, you're the boss!"

## MAKING NEW FRIENDS

I have known many dogs who have overcome their fear of strangers by using this method. It has taken some time, but it has always been worth the effort, because eventually the dog relaxes and, despite his early trauma, he learns to accept people who exhibit a friendly attitude. As the dog's owner, important elements in this rehabilitation process are your positive attitude toward your dog, your patience and understanding, plus your willingness to help your dog become an active part of your lifestyle by giving him the long-overdue experiences that contribute to his self-confidence and friendliness to others.

yard. They may do things like throw things at the dog, bang things against the fence to create excessive noise or yell and scream every time the dog comes near the fence to see them. In short, they exhibit antisocial behavior toward the dog, and he responds accordingly because he feels threatened by them.

The second reason that dogs sometimes act aggressively toward children is that the dogs have never been exposed to babies or children. In this instance, when such a dog encounters children, the dog is puzzled and concerned because the children are small, usually noisy and often very active as they run and play. Crying children often serve to incite the chase instinct in certain dogs because they mistakenly see the wailing children as prey. This more commonly occurs in some of the larger working breeds, but it can also apply to small dogs who mistake children for vermin that need to be caught.

Regardless of the reason, planned and controlled exposure to children over a long period of time can often overcome this problem. As before, begin in a quiet environment with one child holding some tasty treat. Do not allow the child to make any eye contact with the dog, as this will serve as a dominant gesture to the dog. You should stand beside the child and hold the child's hand out with an open palm. The dog may approach the child and take the treat. Be sure the child does not move during the dog's investigation of the treat. Talk softly to the dog, assuring him that all is well and that he's being very good. When he takes the treat, you and the child should verbally praise the dog, but not pet him.

Slowly build up this scenario until you can introduce other children in the same manner and have the dog begin to investigate the children and act pleased to see them. Remember, you're teaching the dog that having children come to see him is just great because they praise him and give him special treats.

Create pleasant experiences for the dog that will eventually wipe away memories of unpleasant encounters with children. Finally, be sure that you train the children how to behave around dogs. Teaching children how to interact with dogs is as important as teaching dogs how to interact with children!

Many dogs are natural protectors of children and watch over their precious charges. Regardless, while this makes for an adorable picture, it's not wise to leave a child of any age and dog unsupervised.

### AGGRESSION TOWARD OTHER DOGS AND OTHER ANIMALS

Spaying the female or neutering the male is the first step needed to correct aggression toward other dogs or other animals. It has been scientifically proven that altered dogs make calmer, more gentle pets that tend to stay close to their homes and owners rather than wandering the streets in search of other canine companions. In addition, altered dogs are less likely to fight with other dogs or to chase or threaten other pet animals such as cats, rabbits, gerbils, birds, etc.

Since aggressive behavior can become a learned habit over a prolonged period of time, it is most effective to neuter or spay as early in the dog's life as possible. In addition, neutering males and spaying females prevents the birth of unwanted litters of puppies. Your veterinarian will advise you regarding the optimal age for altering your pet. Whatever the recommendation, do not postpone altering a dog of appropriate age that shows obvious signs of becoming aggressive.

Next, eliminate any opportunities the dog may have for biting. Keep the dog on lead and never give him the chance to act in a threatening manner toward any

### PREVENTATIVE PRECAUTIONS

By the way, never leave your dog in a fenced yard unless you are there with him to control any situation that may arise when children and adults come within range of the yard and your dog. Preventing troublesome situations is far easier than trying to correct the damage after the fact. One other important matter: never leave a child or children alone with a dog. Adult supervision is essential for controlling the interactions between the two and creating a lifetime of positive experiences for both dog and child.

animal. Finally, begin a planned program of desensitizing the dog so that he begins to like the other animal rather than dislike it. For example, if your dog acts aggressively toward a neighbor's dog, ask the neighbor to put his dog on lead and meet you and your dog on the sidewalk in front of your homes. Have a pocketful of treats with you and use the food to create a pleasant experience for your dog whenever he sees the other dog.

Try this when your dog is hungry and you have some special treats to give him. As you stand on the sidewalk, waiting for your neighbor to appear with his dog, get your dog's attention with a treat in your hand and praise him for watching you. Give him the treat and ask your neighbor to stop about 15 or 20 feet in front of you. When he does, be sure your dog is still watching you. Give the dog another treat and praise him for sitting quietly beside you without lunging toward the neighbor's dog.

As the distance between you and your dog and your neighbor and his dog decreases, you must continue to reward your dog for non-aggressive behavior. The goal here is to teach your dog that seeing his neighbor's dog is very good because every time he sees the other dog, he gets rewarded. Eventually, he will look forward to having the other dog around because it's so beneficial to him.

**KEEP YOUR DISTANCE**
If your dog's aggression is so strong that he goes crazy immediately upon seeing the other dog, ask the neighbor to stop, get your dog under control and, when your dog sits and looks at you, reward him lavishly. Do not attempt to hurry the process of the approaching neighbor and dog until your dog will control himself when they are at a great distance.

It is often tempting to correct the dog's aggressive behavior by jerking on the lead, yelling "No" at your dog or even hitting him. However, studies have shown over and over that punishment for aggressive behavior usually begets more aggression. A slow, deliberate and well-thought-out plan of rehabilitation can prove successful in many cases of dog aggression. However, in cases of extreme aggression, it would be wise to consult a dog behaviorist who can guide you in corrective training. If veterinary help is indicated, the behaviorist will advise you accordingly.

As for aggression toward other animals, cats are often mentioned as being the target of dog chases. What most people fail to notice is that cats frequently instigate these chases by teasing the dogs. If you have a dog that chases your cat, observe their behavior toward each other for a while. Notice how

### FELINE FRENZY

In most cases, your worries about your cat's and dog's play-chasing are unfounded. The cat really likes the dog and enjoys their little games of chase. The dog finds the cat stimulating and looks forward to the interaction and resulting excitement. You are the only one who finds the whole event exhausting and sometimes traumatic when furniture gets shoved out of place or objects get knocked off tables, etc.

the cat may jump up onto a table or counter and sit there in a sprint position, waiting to get the dog's attention. Or the cat may slowly and teasingly strut past the dog as the dog is resting and minding his own business. Then there's the cat who raises her tail, brushes against the dog with an arched back and even purrs invitingly to arouse the dog's interest.

Is it any wonder, then, that the dog will eventually respond and return the cat's attention by chasing the feline? Or he'll declare an all-out chase around the house, complete with his barking and the cat's squealing. As the cat leaps over furniture and around corners, the dog remains in hot pursuit while you stand helplessly, watching this game play out amid your furniture and breakable belongings.

You'll notice that nobody gets hurt during these outbreaks, but you frequently wonder if the day will come when the dog will injure or kill the cat. Then, of course, you worry that they will do permanent damage to your home one of these days. If the cat has been declawed, your worries intensify because you reason that the cat can't protect herself against an attacking dog.

Provided there's no bloodshed during these episodes, you can work with the dog to desensitize him to the cat's advances. Providing more interesting toys for the cat will usually help reduce the feline's desire to get the dog to play.

Again, you will use special food treats to divert your dog's attention away from the cat and onto you and some acceptable activity. You also must be vigilant in observing the cat so that when she begins to initiate her teasing, you can divert her attention to an exciting new toy. As for the dog, when you see the cat begin to entice the dog, get the dog's attention and reward him with a treat for coming to you. Then quickly produce a favorite toy that he hasn't seen in several days, or even a new toy, and begin playing with him. As the dog focuses on you and the toy, praise him for being attentive to you and give him several treats over the next few minutes.

By this time, the cat's attention should be diverted away from inviting the dog to play chase. Thus the imminent threat of a wild chase has passed and you can let the animals settle down into a normal routine once more. Initially you will need to keep a sharp eye out for potential teasing and subsequent chases, so be prepared to spend some time pet-watching.

Eventually the animals will begin to associate the urge to play and chase with fun games, toys and interacting with you. That's when you'll see them come over and stare at you as if to say, "Hey, let's play!" When this happens, stop whatever you're doing and accommodate them, but, each time, make the playtime a little shorter than the time before. In this way, you'll be weaning them off their dependency on you for entertainment and getting them to entertain themselves with their toys.

In case of a dog that acts aggressively toward other pets such as rabbits or birds, adult supervision is essential. Put the dog on lead so you have total control at all times. Reward the dog when he focuses on you and looks away from the other pet. Do not leave the dog alone in the presence of the other pet. If he insists on being aggressive toward the other pet, use a sharp "No" command and remind him to "Watch me" as you train him to ignore the other animal. A positive emphasis on watching you can prove successful over an extended period of time. However, it takes a lot of patience and time on your part.

## "ONLY DOG"

Many years ago, I had an Airedale that would not or could not tolerate other pets. She attacked several other dogs in the household and made the lives of a cat and a canary absolutely miserable. Finally, after many attempts at retraining her over a period of two years, I gave up. I assigned her to live in the kennel and never come into direct contact with other animals. Several times a week, she and I went out to a large fenced field where I worked her out in obedience exercises and played fetching games with her. I gave her lots of exercise and attention. She lived that way for another eight years, seemingly content to be the "only dog."

## ESTABLISHING DOMINANCE

Having the dog do several five-minute down exercises every day will help to establish people as dominant figures in the dog's world. Having him do a down before he goes for a walk, before being served a meal and before he is allowed to jump up on the furniture (provided you allow him to do this in the first place) are other examples of exercising the human dominance theory to the dog.

yourself to the fact that your dog must be restrained from contact with other animals at all times. You will give the dog jobs to do around the home, such as retrieving his lead when it's time to go for a walk. You will train him in basic obedience so you have a line of communication with the dog; thus, you can let him know that despite his dislike of other animals, you will not tolerate aggressive behavior. And finally, you will give him two or three down exercises every day, which will serve to reinforce your role of leadership to him. A 10-minute down in the morning and a 20- or 30-minute down while you eat your dinner in the evening will get the message across loud and clear.

### DEALING WITH DOG AGGRESSION

When dealing with any form of aggression in a dog, it must be remembered that the safety of all those involved is of primary importance. The dog must be restrained at all times so that he does not have any opportunity at all to bite. It is imperative that the owner be responsible at all times for the safety of other people and animals.

Unfortunately, there are certain dogs that will never give up wanting to go after other animals. For those dogs, the answer lies in your control of the entire situation. You must resign

Never allowing the dog to attain a position of control is paramount. The dog should be kept on his collar and lead whenever he's in the presence of others. In some cases, this means that the dog should be muzzled so that his owner can handle him and he is unable to bite anyone.

Teaching the dog that he must be submissive to his owners and other humans is the most effective way to get the dog to accept his role within his human pack. Dogs and wolves in the wild do not bite superior individuals, because they have learned that their leaders do not tolerate aggressive behavior. The same theory exists when a dog sees his family and other people as superior beings.

The only exception to this rule is the fear-biter. Since the fear-biting dog is aggressive yet afraid, he must be treated with caution and coaxing as previously described. Tranquilizers, used under the supervision of a professional behaviorist and veterinarian, may help the fear-biter to relax and develop self-confidence while interacting with people.

Finally, obedience training should be considered essential to the successful management of all dogs. The dog should be taught to sit, lie down, stay, heel beside his owner without pulling and come when called. This training is the most important element in developing a rewarding relationship between a dog and humans. The cost is usually reasonable and the lessons usually take place over around an eight-week time period, yet the results will last a lifetime.

Sleeve training with a Dogo Argentino. This is a dog with strong protective instincts, which can be directed in a positive or negative manner depending on the training. This type of training should only be done with a professional.

# BARKING

There are many reasons why a dog barks. Though the cause of the noise may be different in different dogs, the effect it has on the humans who hear it is the same. A short, crisp bark may get our attention, but consistent barking can quickly turn to pure annoyance. And since the sounds of a barking dog are heard by not only the owner but also by all those within hearing range, the barking can quickly escalate into a public nuisance.

However, there are certain times and circumstances when the bark of a dog is a welcome and reassuring sound, such as warning of approaching danger, the smoke of a fire, the presence of a stranger or the whimper of a sick child. These are all occasions when a dog's bark can avert disaster. Therefore it would be extremely unwise to condemn a dog for barking before we learn why he is doing it.

There are four basic categories into which barking falls: alerting, attention-getting, communication and excitement. Let's look at these in more detail to determine the correct course of action that an owner should use in response to each type of barking.

## WHY DOES A DOG BARK?

### ALERTING
Drawing attention to a strange person, animal, object, sound, sight or smell can all be causes of a dog's alerting by barking. Barking can also be a precursor to a fearful retreat or a prelude to an offensive attack.

*Case A:* In the case of your dog's trying to alert you to something new and strange, let the animal investigate the source. Go with him to see what he's barking about. Do not stroke, pet or coddle him in any way at this time, and don't prolong the investigation. When you determine that the source of the dog's concern is harmless, quickly divert his attention to some activity he enjoys, such as a fetching game or a play session with a favorite toy. Be matter-of-fact and focus on the harmlessness of the source by acting in a natural manner. Smile, laugh, be happy and touch the person or object in question so the dog sees that it does not represent a threat. The more casual you are in circumstances such as this, the quicker your dog will be to cease his worry and concern.

*Case B:* In the case of a stranger, praise the dog for alerting you to the person's presence. Many dogs, for example, react aggressively toward delivery personnel. When a delivery person comes to your door, act happily and assure the dog that the person is a friend. Have the dog on lead when you go to the door and have him sit beside you as you greet the person. Give the delivery person a biscuit and ask him or her to give it to your dog as soon as you give the signal.

Be firm with the dog and have him sit quietly beside you without barking or lunging at the person. As soon as you get the dog under control, change your tone of voice to one of friendliness and indicate to the dog that this person is a nice one. Once the dog shows signs of calming down and accepting the person's presence at the door, have the person give the dog the biscuit. Do not have the person pet the dog at this time. Simply praise the dog for being a good boy and behaving in a polite manner.

After several encounters like this, you will see a change in how your dog accepts the delivery

This dog's warning bark says loud and clear, "Stay away."

The white dog is communicating with his bark that he wants to come into the yard.

person once you give the "OK" signal that the person is friendly. When this occurs, you can begin to let the person pet the dog as the dog sits politely by your side. However, when you get to this stage of training, be firm with the dog so he clearly understands that polite acceptance is the only behavior that will be tolerated. Praise generously when he does this.

*Case C:* In the case that the stranger is not welcome at your door or on your property, praise the dog for alerting you to his presence and then deal with the stranger in an appropriate manner. Do not expect the dog to exercise polite manners with someone who

is not welcome in your home, but be sure that you have control of the dog at all times, because a dog that threatens people and/or bites them is not acceptable.

*Case D:* In the case of a fearful dog who barks as a precursor to retreating from a situation, you can usually predict this by the animal's behavior. Not only will he give warning of his fearfulness by barking in short, high-pitched yipping-type barks, he will probably tuck his tail between his legs and lay his ears flat against his head. He may also turn away and present a side view to the perceived source of his fear.

When a dog is afraid, it is unwise and dangerous to pursue

the dog or try to pet him. If the dog is on lead, you can use the lead to guide him away from the scene that's causing him concern. Do not coddle or console him. Instead, talk softly and casually so he begins to relax and refocus his attention on something else. You can encourage this refocusing by using familiar words and phrases that he will recognize as things he enjoys, such as taking a walk or playing with a favorite toy.

In the case of a dog that is demonstrating fearfulness while he's not on lead, you have less control to guide him into a less stressful position. Talking and slowly moving away from what is making him afraid, toward something he knows and likes, may be your only solution. As soon as the dog is away from the source of his fear, try to get him hooked up to his lead so you have more control.

*Case E:* As a warning before an offensive attack, barking is usually loud and deep-throated, rather than the lighter-toned fearful bark. The dog will be standing so that the bulk of his weight is on his front quarters and you can see him leaning forward. His ears will be erect, his tail held up and rigidly, and he will show his teeth with each bark.

If you ever see a dog behind a fence, warning a stranger to stay away, his whole body is saying, "Get out of here now!" That

message is quite clear to everyone who sees the dog. Never try to approach a dog displaying these behaviors, as it's almost certain that you will be bitten if you disregard his warning. Turn sideways to the dog, do not give him any eye contact and slowly walk away. Running will only incite him to more aggression. Threatening signals from a dog are meant to be respected and believed.

Outdoor barking could be to alert the owner that someone is passing by, or it could be a warning to the passerby to keep on going.

ATTENTION-GETTING

When an owner deliberately spoils a dog or unintentionally rewards him for barking, the dog quickly learns how to get attention. For example, a dog barks because he is startled, and the owner reaches down and pets the dog to assure him that all is well. The dog perceives the petting and consoling as a reward for barking. Thus he barks whenever he wants attention.

Attention-getting barking can be corrected, provided that the owner is determined to "unspoil" the dog. Let's create a fictitious scenario and the solution to the problem it produces. This problem is common to small dogs and their owners.

As a puppy, the dog frequently barked and jumped up on the owner to get the owner's attention. The owner would bend down and pick up the puppy. Soon the puppy learned that whenever he wanted the owner's attention, all he had to do was bark and jump up on his owner.

Well, by the time the puppy reaches adulthood, the habit has been formed and the dog constantly demands that his owner pick him up and carry him around. The owner finds this annoying, yet he loves the little dog, so he hesitates to reprimand him. Instead the owner tries yelling at the dog, but to no avail. The dog continues to jump and the owner continues to try various tactics to correct the problem, yet nothing positive comes of the owner's attempts.

The solution to this problem is to let the dog know that it's fine to ask for attention, but in an acceptable manner. The dog must learn that, as with most things in life, there is a price to pay for that

## SEPARATION ANXIETY

Separation anxiety is a major cause of a dog's barking. When a dog is left alone, he can experience such a high level of frustration due to being separated from his master (pack or family) that he barks almost constantly to alleviate the anxiety he feels about being alone. In turn, this behavior gets the owner's attention, and although it may be unpleasant attention, it is better than no attention at all.

attention. Instead of immediately responding to the dog's request that he be picked up, the owner now has the dog do something to earn his attention. Once the dog begins to realize that attention is no longer free, he can be trained to remain on the floor and accept attention from there rather than from the owner's arms.

If you experience a similar problem, teach the dog to sit on command. Then, when he comes to you and demands your attention, have him sit before you respond to him. When he obeys the sit command, you can give him some attention. At first, you can pick him up, pet and praise him briefly and then return him to the floor. If he barks and jumps on you again, have him sit again. Follow his sit with praise again, but this time don't pick him up. Instead, bend down and pet him as he sits in front of you.

Soon the dog will learn that he must do something before he will receive your attention. In other words, ignoring behavior you don't want and recognizing behavior you do want will produce positive results. Responding to behavior you don't want is perceived by the dog as acceptance, and he'll continue to do it forever. However, when he learns that you'll only recognize him for good behavior, he'll exercise that good behavior in order to receive your attention.

## ATTEMPTS TO COMMUNICATE

The dog, being a social animal, needs to communicate with his pack (humans or other dogs). He uses barking as a means to gain food, water, shelter and comfort. Many dogs, for instance, will give several sharp barks at their owners a few minutes before their regularly scheduled mealtimes. A dog will often give several short, sharp barks as an invitation to other dogs or people to play. When a dog is left outside in a fenced area and his pack members (his family) are inside, he will frequently stand at the door and bark to communicate his desire to be let inside to join them.

However, sometimes, as we've mentioned earlier, an owner reacts inappropriately to barking and the dog reads the owner's actions as something good that he'd like repeated. Let's say that the dog brings a toy to you and drops it at your feet. Then he stands there

**This type of body language is often accompanied by excited barking and means one thing: "I want to play!"**

A dog can't see what's going on on the other side of a privacy fence, but he certainly can hear and smell, so he will bark to vocalize that he knows something's out there.

barking and looking up at you. Without thinking, you pick up the toy and toss it across the room. That behavior signals a message to the dog that you're willing to play with him whenever he asks. Of course, this will not always be convenient, yet you've taught the dog that standing in front of you and barking will get you to play with him regardless of what you're doing at the time.

This behavior is usually found in a high-energy dog who is bored and has nothing to do. At this point, you have two choices. The first choice is to respond to the dog's demand by throwing the toy for him. This response will probably escalate into a whole series of tossing and retrieving. One toss is usually never enough!

The second choice is to acknowledge the dog's boredom and, before you toss the toy, have the dog do something for you. A sit or a down/stay would be appropriate. Once the dog complies with your command, praise him and then toss the toy. If he brings the toy back to you and begins barking again, repeat the procedure so that each time he demands your attention, he must earn it by doing something first. Very shortly he'll decide that he doesn't want to be bothered with doing something just so you'll throw the toy. He'll soon find something else to do and wander off to entertain himself.

## WHAT DO YOU NEED?

When your dog tries to communicate with you through barking, pay attention to him. He's probably trying to tell you something that is important to him. For example, he's hungry, he's thirsty and his water bowl is empty, he's too cold or too warm or he's trying to do something that requires your help (go out to relieve himself, get a toy that's out of his reach, tell you that a family member has just pulled into the driveway, etc.). Provided that his needs are legitimate, barking should be considered acceptable; provided that you see to his needs, he'll be quick to stop barking.

To be fair to the dog, if he enjoys retrieving, he should be given ample opportunities to play fetch with you at your convenience. Once he understands that you'll play the fetch game with him, he'll be a lot less likely to pester you when it's not convenient for you to play with him.

For the very stubborn dog who will not give up, you can always give him some time out in his crate, say five or ten minutes. Once released from time out, praise him lightly and return to your previous activity as you ignore the dog. Sooner or later, he will learn that getting you to do something he wants does not come without a price. He either obeys your commands or finds

*Enjoy your puppy's quiet period—he will find his voice soon enough. Min Pins have quite a bit to say!*

himself in time out, neither of which he cares to do.

As time goes by and with proper responses to his behavior, he'll develop habits that suit you and satisfy him as well. Playing a game of fetch with a toy is fun when you are the one who initiates the game or when the dog brings you his toy and sits quietly until you can play with him. For sure, he'll learn that barking unnecessarily gets him nowhere.

### EXCITEMENT

Dogs verbalize their emotions much as people do. For example, they often bark during play when they get very excited. They also bark when they're anticipating something that excites them, such as a game of fetch, a special doggie treat or going out for a walk with his owner. Frustration also can create barking in a dog.

Let's say the dog wants to play with a favorite toy that is in his sight but out of his reach. He may attempt to get the toy but, when those efforts fail, he may stand there and stare at the toy while he barks incessantly until someone comes to retrieve the toy for him.

If you can determine the cause of the barking, you should allow it for a reasonable amount of time. Lowering the level of excitement usually lowers the bark reflex, and you usually can control this. When you wish to quiet the dog, change the cause of his excitement to a more calming activity. As soon as the barking lessens, praise the dog with "Good quiet." In the case of frustration, lessen his barking by alleviating the dog's frustration or removing the dog from the cause of his frustration.

It's beneficial to both dogs and people that dog owners understand the causes and appropriate human responses to barking. Often when small dogs bark they are sounding an alarm. Big dogs, on the other hand, bark to issue a warning and/or threat. When people respond appropriately to barking, they generally set the pattern for the barking to subside yet recur when necessary. Conversely, responding inappropriately usually escalates the barking and thereby solicits more barking.

In short, with barking or other of their dogs' behavior, owners should recognize positive behavior and ignore or divert negative behavior. Remember, behaviors that bring pleasant results tend to be repeated, whereas behaviors that bring on unpleasant results are usually not repeated. To a dog, being ignored is most unpleasant, so the dog quickly figures out that, in order to get pleasant attention, he must repeat certain behaviors (such as not barking unnecessarily) and stop others.

## I'M SO EXCITED!

Barking is a healthy, natural manifestation of excitement. It can be loosely compared to human vocalization in the case of play, anticipation and frustration. Certain breeds are known to have lower levels of bark reflexes than others. Many small dogs are quicker to bark and more likely to bark for longer periods than some large dogs.

# CARSICKNESS

Dogs are most likely to get carsick when they are puppies. With enough practice riding in the family car, they soon overcome this and usually end up loving to go for rides in the car. A mistake often made by owners of young puppies is to only take the pups for car rides when it's time to visit the veterinarian for shots and checkups. The puppy soon relates the vet visit with the car trip and learns to dread the experience. By the time the puppy is an adult dog, he not only hates the veterinarian but he also detests riding in the car!

To avoid this scenario from occurring, train your puppy to enjoy the ride and the visit to the veterinarian, too. First, begin by teaching the puppy to enjoy the trip in the car. Place the puppy in his crate in the back seat of the car and drive around the block. Don't attempt to go any further, and be sure to turn corners gently so the pup doesn't get thrown around in the crate. While you're traveling, talk happily to the puppy and tell him he's a good boy. This will get him to focus on you, not on the motion of the car. As soon as you get back in your driveway, stop the engine and give the puppy a food treat as you praise him for being such a good boy during the ride.

Repeat this process for several days. Then, as the pup begins to relax during the trips, lengthen the ride to two blocks. In a few more days, you should be able to take very short trips around town. As the pup begins to show pleasure during these rides, introduce a short stop and then return home. In this way, you are getting the puppy ready to enjoy trips that include a stop or two.

Once the puppy tolerates short trips, you can make a stop, get out of the car and leave the puppy alone in the car (for a minute or two only). When you return, be sure to praise and reward him with another special treat. In the beginning, make those stops very short and don't go into great detail when leaving the dog. Simply tell him to "Wait here" and get out of the car and walk away. It's your return that should produce the happy talk and reward.

Now it's time to take the pup to visit his veterinarian. Arm yourself with some special treats

Crate training provides many advantages. Once a dog is accustomed to a crate in his home, he will be comfortable with being in a crate wherever the need for safe confinement arises.

Some dogs prefer
alternative modes
of transportation!

and ask the vet to give the treats to the dog as he examines him. This will get the puppy accustomed to being handled by the doctor. If he must give the puppy a shot, have him give the puppy a treat immediately following the procedure. You want the puppy to forget any discomfort associated with the veterinarian and to focus on the kind doctor and his pocketful of treats. A few extra minutes spent teaching the puppy not to fear the veterinarian when he is very young will pay off in big dividends when the dog becomes an adult.

In the case of the adult dog that gets carsick, the same training procedure as described for accustoming the young pup to the car may prove successful. There are also anti-motion-sickness pills

## TRAVEL ALERT

One important matter regarding dogs and cars must be noted here: never leave a dog in a car!! Even if the windows are rolled down on a warm day (65° Fahrenheit and above), a car can heat up to temperatures over 100° in a matter of minutes and the dog will suffocate. With the windows rolled down, it is just as dangerous, because the dog may try to escape and injure himself in the process. In some places, leaving a dog unattended in a car is illegal. Whether legal or not, it is just plain unsafe, no matter what!

available from most veterinarians; these can help the dog tolerate riding in a car. These medications should not be given to a dog without a veterinarian's supervision. When used for motion sickness, they should be eliminated as soon as the dog can be weaned off the medication. You don't want to make the dog dependent on medication for car trips. Using a slow, steady process of getting the dog accustomed to riding in the car because the experience is pleasurable will develop a love of travel for the dog that will last a lifetime.

Sturdy fiberglass crates are good for use during travel and can double as handy carriers for smaller dogs.

Sighthounds, like the Whippet and Rhodesian Ridgeback, have strong prey-chase instincts that are easily incited. In dog racing, the dogs are lured around the course in pursuit of a mechanical rabbit or similar "prey."

# CHASING

## CHASING CHILDREN

Dogs chase things because they possess a hereditary instinct to hunt. Dogs are carnivores and, as such, they must learn how to hunt at an early age. The fact that we have domesticated dogs and we provide them with food does not erase the instinct that was bred into them many years ago.

Furthermore, some breeds are more chase-oriented than others. Terriers, for example, were bred to chase and even go underground to catch moles, mice and other vermin. Consequently, things that move quickly simulate prey to terriers. When a terrier sees something that moves quickly, he

What's more fun to chase than a littermate?

immediately thinks "catch and destroy," and the chase is on!

Some large breeds of dog, such as the German Shepherd, Rottweiler, Doberman Pinscher, Bouvier des Flandres and Giant Schnauzer, are bred to be natural guard dogs. The trait of pursuing and catching fleeing trespassers, felons, etc., comes naturally to them. In addition, they are big enough and powerful enough to stop a person who is attempting to escape.

In the case of chasing children, the big guard-type breeds see running and squealing children as prey. First, the sound of children squealing in play or crying in distress arouses the guard dog. He searches for the source of the sound and, when he finds it and it is running, his instinct to chase

### TERRIER CHASE INSTINCT

When the object of the chase is a child, the terrier's instinct goes into play long before his training and domestication are able to signal "false alarm—wrong kind of prey." Thus the terrier will frequently nip at the ankles of running, squealing children as they play their childhood games. While this is not life-threatening, it is painful. After all, a bite is a bite, and it must not be allowed to occur.

and restrain his "prey" is engaged. This is extremely dangerous and must never be allowed to occur. If you are the owner of a large working dog with strong chase instincts, it is your responsibility to keep the dog under control at all times. There must never be an opportunity for the dog to chase, catch and eventually bite a child.

In some cases of child-chasing, the dog can be programed to participate in an alternative activity such as fetching games, chewing on favorite bones or something else he enjoys whenever the child in question behaves in an active, noisy manner. In families where there are small children, it is wise to obtain the family dog as a puppy rather than as an adult dog and let the puppy become accustomed to the children as they grow up together. The dogs for which the alternate-behavior method is successful are usually non-guarding-type dogs of any size, which were originally bred to be companions, hunting dogs or

*Watching a dog run about in the yard, it's sometimes hard to tell what piques his interest and arouses his desire to chase.*

dogs intended to work with their masters as helpers. Dogs of this nature can be found in the Toy, Sporting, Non-Sporting and Hound Groups.

In the case of mild chasing syndrome, behavior modification should consist of having the dog under control and exposing the dog to various situations in which a child is running and playing noisily. Have the dog look at you whenever the child comes near, and reward the dog for his attention with special food treats. After giving the dog a food treat, engage him in a fun activity to divert his attention away from the child and onto something he enjoys, such as retrieving a ball.

Repeat this training often and watch for signs that the dog is beginning to associate the playing child with his own rewarding and fun activity. At some point, you might even have the child throw the ball for the dog. That way, the dog begins to get the idea that the playing child is something fun for the dog as well, rather than something he should chase.

**CHASING MOVING VEHICLES**
There are two possible reasons why some dogs chase vehicles. The first involves the natural chase instinct to hunt, such as previously described. The second involves the dog's urge to fend off what he perceives as intruders to his home and property. In other

words, he's acting in a defensive mode.

Training to stop a dog from chasing vehicles can be successful with some dogs, but not with others. It depends on the degree of chase desire in the dog and the amount and type of training that the owner employs.

If your dog likes to chase cars, put the dog on lead and take him out to your front yard. When you see a car approaching, walk with the dog toward the street. When you get about three or four feet from the sidewalk, turn abruptly, yell some startling comment such as "Watch out!" and run back and away from the approaching vehicle. When you reach a safe distance from the street, praise the dog and give him a food treat.

Repeat this procedure until the time comes when your dog begins to instinctively turn back and away from approaching vehicles. Always praise your dog and reward him with a treat so that he learns that avoiding an approaching vehicle, rather than chasing it, is a rewarding thing to do.

I have known several people who have purchased water pistols, which they bring with them in their cars, and they squirt water in the faces of dogs that chase their cars. This should be done only with the dog's owner controlling the dog while the driver moves very slowly past the dog. This should never be attempted with a

**UNSAFE AND ILLEGAL**
The consequences of chasing any moving vehicle can be devastating, even fatal. Since most communities have leash laws, dogs should not be permitted to roam freely at any time. Even without such laws, it is unwise to allow your dog to be outdoors without some form of constraint. If you want the dog to enjoy more freedom than the average leash allows, you can purchase a 50-foot-long line to use whenever you want the dog to exercise but still be under your control.

driver who is not fully aware of what the dog's owner is trying to accomplish. Driving too close to the dog, driving too fast, driving in an erratic pattern and the like can injure or kill the dog, so every safety measure must be established before this set-up is attempted. Never use this water-pistol method from a bicycle or motorcycle, as the dog will have a full view of the driver and learn to dislike that person. The driver of a car is usually sufficiently hidden so that the dog will not associate the water in his face with the driver.

Be aware that not all dogs can be trained to avoid chasing moving objects. Keeping the dog under physical control at all times will always prove to be the safest way to manage your dog and prevent accidents from happening.

All settled in for a
good chew!

# CHEWING

There are two basic reasons why dogs chew. Interestingly, they are the same two reasons why humans chew as well: physical and emotional. In all cases, the reason why the dog is chewing must be determined before a solution to the problem can be initiated. Disciplining the dog is usually not the correct route to take in eliminating the problem; the reaction to the discipline usually initiates more chewing or some other undesirable behavior. Thus, eliminating the cause will solve the problem while it eases the dog's frustrations.

For example, when the puppy chews on your hands, there are two easy ways to stop that behavior without creating more problems. First, keep your hands away from the puppy's face. By keeping your hands behind the dog's line of peripheral vision, he will not attempt to chew on your hands. Pet him around the shoulder area and keep any stimulation to chew away from his mouth. Second, if he seeks out your hands to chew anyway, spray your hands with a product such as bitter apple or a similar deterrent.

This type of product is designed to make the forbidden object taste unpleasant and, thus, to make chewing on it undesirable.

Puppies chew when they are teething. Their jaws ache with pain when the new teeth are breaking through bone or flesh. This usually occurs prior to the age of 16 weeks and can extend up to about 20 weeks of age. When the molars come through at about eight months of age, the puppy will chew again, but this time he will gnaw at the back of his mouth on hard items (such as chair legs!).

Once teething is over, there is rarely a repeat of this type of chewing behavior. However, it is beneficial to both puppy and owner to know exactly what kind of objects the dog prefers during his chewing stages. Chewing on ice cubes is soothing for puppies during all stages of teething. The older puppy needs hard objects to chew because his back molars are coming in and his gums ache with pain. Gnawing on bones or hard nylon chew toys helps relieve some of this discomfort. For the young pup who is losing the baby teeth in the front of his mouth, he needs soft items such as stuffed toys, old towels tied in knots or any type of soft, safe material that he can sink his baby teeth into for relief.

Most often the puppy will swallow his baby teeth during the course of eating a meal or the teeth will fall out as he chews on a toy. Only occasionally will human intervention be necessary in removing a baby tooth. This may happen when the first canine teeth refuse to fall out yet the permanent canine teeth are already pushing through the gums. In that case, your veterinarian can remove the baby canines during a regular office visit. It is important that the baby canines come out to allow the permanent canines to come in straight and properly, so check your puppy's mouth frequently

**Puppy teeth can be found most anywhere, so don't be surprised at what your pup finds chewable.**

> ## TOOTH FAIRY
> Again, the loss of baby teeth usually occurs around 16 weeks of age, but it can vary with different breeds and different individuals within a specific breed. The best way to know when the puppy is beginning to lose his baby teeth is to check his mouth regularly. You may see loose teeth just waiting to fall out, or you may see teeth that are still in the socket but very loose when you touch them.

once he reaches that four-month milestone.

Emotional chewing is a different matter. Again, like humans, dogs often chew due to emotional problems as numerous as the dogs themselves. If we think about human examples of worry and frustration and how we react to them, we realize that we use our mouths to alleviate the anxiety we feel. We smoke, we eat, we chew gum, we talk incessantly, we bite our fingernails, children suck their thumbs and so on. These are all things that people may do to relieve stress.

For dogs, chewing becomes the manifestation of anxieties caused by situations in their environments. These situations can be anything from isolation frustration (in which the dog is left alone and is very insecure about the situation) to chewing caused by excitement or nervous-

ness. I've known young puppies who get so excited when guests come to the home that they grab anything within their reach and begin chewing on it: pillows, articles of clothing hanging over the side of a chair, pairs of shoes or slippers, magazines, newspapers. They don't seem to care what the articles are; their only concern is to get something chewable into their mouths.

Generally this early-life "excitement chewing" usually subsides by the time the puppy is eight months of age. In some small breeds, it will disappear by six months of age. Regardless, be patient with your puppy. Keep him occupied with items on which he is permitted to chew and direct his energy to manifest his excitement harmlessly rather than with forbidden objects. If you simply grab a forbidden item

away from him without providing him with an acceptable alternative, he will become so frustrated that he'll probably chew on something even more harmful than his original choice.

Chewing to get your attention is another scenario in which redirection is the way to correct the problem. Sometimes the dog will become jealous of your attention toward another pet or a person in the family. He will become frustrated and, unable to express his anxiety, he'll begin chewing on some forbidden object. By noticing this behavior and making a fuss about it, you are teaching the dog that chewing on a particular item will get your attention, even though it's negative rather than positive attention. As we've mentioned, to a dog, any kind of attention is better than no attention.

**Some dogs are more oral than others, with the retrievers topping the list. Retriever breeds love to play fetching games, and they often have favorite toys that they carry around with them.**

## ACCEPTABLE CHEWING

I know of one Golden Retriever who, when he hears the doorbell ring, runs to fetch an old cotton gardening glove that his owner gave him. He carries it proudly to the door to show the guest his "pretty," and he's been doing that since he was a puppy! In fact, when he's very excited, he will even carry the glove outdoors when he goes for a walk! This is a harmless yet satisfying behavior that he's been doing all his life, and it proves to be a behavior that his owner graciously accepts.

Instead of correcting the dog, have him do something for you. Tell him to get a favorite toy or do a down/stay or a sit/stay. When he complies, praise him for being a good dog. As long as he feels you're recognizing him, he'll be content and secure as he waits while you turn your attention to someone or something else. Again, recognize the behavior you want and redirect his energy toward positive, rather than negative, things.

Now, let's turn our attention to isolation frustration chewing, which is a very common problem with dogs and one that can be controlled if approached properly.

If you attempt to alter the behavior incorrectly, disastrous results are almost sure to occur. Here again, understanding the cause of the chewing problem is the key to solving it.

Being a social animal, the dog needs and wants to live in a pack. He is not meant to live alone and would not survive on his own in the wild. Just think about wolves and how they manage to survive. They hunt in packs and rely on the help and cooperation of other pack members for success and survival. Dogs have carried those genes into the domestic age from the time when they were wolves. They are still social animals and

**Puppies love to sink their aching gums into soft toys to relieve the pain of teething, and soft toys also provide them with cuddly friends with whom they can snuggle.**

Although dogs might argue that they are perfectly tasty, branches and sticks do not make suitable chew toys. The splinters are too dangerous.

**WHERE ARE YOU?**
When you go off to work in the morning and leave your dog alone in the house to wander aimlessly around all day, the dog becomes worried, anxious, frustrated. "Where," he wonders, "is my pack? Why did they leave me? When will they return or will they return at all?" On the other hand, use of a crate makes the dog feel secure while prohibiting him from destructive chewing and other undesirable behavior caused by separation anxiety.

worried that his pack has abandoned him, so he begins to chew to alleviate the anxiety he feels. Unfortunately, what he chooses to chew on makes no difference to him. As long as it's available, he'll chew it!

Let's say, for example, that he's resting on your sofa when the urge to chew overtakes him. He isn't likely to jump off the sofa and go fetch a dog bone to chew on. Instead, he'll begin chewing on the sofa cushion or the arm of the sofa. Before you know it, he's made a huge hole in the sofa and the stuffing is beginning to come out. The stuffing then is a new and interesting material that will further pique his curiosity, and he'll proceed to pull more stuffing from the hole.

By the time you get home at the end of the day, your living room looks like a disaster area and your sofa is damaged beyond repair. You realize that the dog is responsible for the damage, so you begin to discipline him. You yell and scream, you may even hit him; you show your disapproval in a variety of ways. Whatever your reaction to the devastation, the dog reads your fury as a consequence of your coming home. Thus he quickly learns that your arrival at the end of the day will mean that he will be reprimanded. Because he did his chewing earlier in the day, he'll never associate the destruction of

do not do well when isolated from the pack, whether that pack consists of other dogs or humans.

Just as with humans, worry leads to stress and that, in turn, creates a need for the dog to relieve this stress by way of some physical activity. The dog is

Prevent boredom, and the destructive behavior that can go with it, by spending time with your dog, engaging him in active play with his toys.

## IDLE PAWS

Without a doubt, the single most important factor in dogs' chewing is that they can. They have the time, the energy, the objects and, to them, the reason. The smart owner realizes this and manages the dog and his activities creatively to prevent unwanted behaviors and to bring pleasure to him and his dog in their lives together.

Having a small confined area or "cubby" in which to rest will provide him with that security. Giving him a small safe place in which to make himself comfortable and wait for your return will prevent his doing damage to your property and to himself. If he should ever chew an electrical cord, for example, he could electrocute himself and/or set the house on fire! The chapter on house-training includes complete house- and crate-training instructions for both puppies and adult dogs. In addition, it contains an explanation of how the dog perceives his confined area and why he needs his own space.

Chewing can be caused by an infinite number of reasons. However, the solution to correcting undesirable chewing lies with understanding the reason that the dog is chewing. Maybe you've recently moved to a new home and the dog is unsure of where he is and why he isn't being taken back to the home to which he's accustomed. Maybe one of the members of your family has gone away for an extended time and the dog keeps waiting for that person to return. Perhaps you've acquired another pet, such as a cat or a bird, even another dog. Maybe there's a new baby in your house and the dog now has to take second place while this new strange "thing" is taking center stage around the house.

the couch with the punishment and scolding.

Since you can't stay home in order to prevent the dog from chewing forbidden items around the house, you must prevent destructive chewing before it ever starts. Crate training is the most obvious, safest way to do that. Remember that your dog is a social creature and he needs to feel secure within his pack.

No matter what the reason for the dog's stress and/or concern, his chewing problem must be directed to acceptable chewing rather than to random, often unacceptable, chewing. In addition, other activities must take the place of some of his former chewing behavior. In this case (and in the case of some other undesirable behaviors, too), you, the owner, must use your creative imagination to find ways to alleviate the dog's trauma before his unacceptable chewing becomes such a habit that it lasts a lifetime and becomes a serious threat to you and the dog.

A busy dog has little time for destructive activities. A dog that gets regular physical exercise is less likely to waste energy on chewing and other unacceptable behaviors. Daily exercise of running, jogging or walking is a healthy way for both you and your

Direct your dog to proper chew objects until he gets the idea, because it's inevitable that initially he will find forbidden objects more interesting to sink his teeth into.

This is not an example of productive chewing behavior. His attempts to chew through the metal are futile, causing further frustration, not to mention how dangerous this can be.

dog to avoid boredom. Plenty of activity prevents idle time from creating worry and frustration to dominate your dog's life. Also be sure that your dog has a variety of toys on which he's allowed to chew. If he starts to chew on a forbidden item, redirect him to his own chew toys.

A dog whose owner gives him excessive attention for undesirable chewing will interpret that to mean that all he has to do to get his owner's attention is to chew some forbidden article. Therefore, don't coddle your dog. Never give him attention for unwanted behavior or you will only get more unwanted behavior! Make the dog understand that he must earn your affection, not simply

demand it. A dog that participates in some form of sporting activity such as obedience trialing, tracking, dog-show competition, agility or backpacking will have little reason to find an alternative activity like chewing.

One other important element in successful management of your dog is to always be generous with praise. Recognize his good traits and behaviors. When he pleases you, let him know! Simple things like saying "Good boy" and petting him will go a long way in rewarding desirable behavior. Remember, a behavior that results in a pleasant event tends to be repeated, so praise your dog often while letting his unwanted behavior die of neglect.

Rope toys have dental advantages for dogs, acting like floss as they chew and also aiding in the loss of puppy teeth.

You must keep your yard clean, and that means always picking up droppings. You don't want your dog to discover a mess while sniffing around.

# COPROPHAGIA

Stool eating is not uncommon in dogs and puppies, although admittedly it is most unpleasant to humans. Mother dogs eat the stool of their babies before the little ones can walk and defecate on their own. Stray dogs will often eat the stool of other dogs and animals, as well as their own. Pet dogs frequently eat the stool of the cats with whom they live. That's why cat owners are urged to keep litter boxes out of the reach of their dogs!

If diet is not the problem, there are several steps to take to stop the dog from eating stool. First, make sure that the dog's diet is consistent in quantity and quality. Second, be sure to feed the dog twice a day rather than just once. This will prevent the dog from ever feeling excessively hungry; thus, he won't get the urge to eat stool. Finally, don't punish or scold the dog for eating stool. When you see stool on the ground, take him away from the area immediately. Distract him from thinking about the stool by initiating an enjoyable activity such as playing a game of fetch or going for a walk.

Keep the dog's relief area and your entire yard free of stool, and don't give him the opportunity to eat the stool of other animals. You should always clean up immediately after your dog relieves himself, but never let him see you clean up stool. If he sees you paying attention to the stool, he may mistake this as a sign that you want him to pay more attention to it as well.

Most cases of coprophagia can be corrected in a period of several months. Some dogs can take longer to cure of the habit and some dogs can never be corrected. If you own a dog that cannot be corrected, you will need to be vigilant about prevention for the dog's entire life. However, hopefully your dog will respond to your correcting the problem. Regardless, be assured that coprophagia is not unusual and that your dog is normal.

**Ah, the mysteries of the cat's litter box that compel a dog to explore!**

# DIGGING

**Some dogs are good at hiding their bad habits.**

A dog's digging in the ground can be destructive, harmless, annoying, comical, a plain nuisance or any and all of these things! It all depends on the owner's perspective and the type of digging. Digging in plain soil is one thing; digging in a prized rose garden is quite another!

One thing is for sure when dealing with a dog who digs: just as with other behaviors, understanding the reason for the dog's digging is the key to controlling and/or altering the behavior. At the outset, it must be understood that eliminating an undesirable behavior may force the dog to replace the unwanted behavior with an equally undesirable one.

Even more importantly, eliminating an undesirable behavior with the use of punishment is rarely the correct and successful answer to the problem. The punishment frequently causes the dog to become frustrated, so, again, the behavior increases rather than decreases.

There are, however, two possibilities that can change the course of the dog's actions and, at the same time, satisfy the owner's need to eliminate the behavior. First, the owner can replace the unwanted behavior with a desirable one. Second, the owner can alter the behavior enough so the digging becomes acceptable.

## WHY DO DOGS DIG?

Now let's look at some of the most common reasons for digging and the cures for these problems.

### DIGGING TO RETRIEVE A BURIED OBJECT

If you have no objection to his doing so, allow the dog to dig up the object. A dog will often bury bones, toys and articles he wishes to hide. Naturally, he will bury these items in soft earth rather than hard ground if at all possible. Then, one day when you least expect it, he will come marching into the house with a dirt-covered item that you had long forgotten about.

If there is a reason why the dog should not be allowed to retrieve the object, you should remove the dog from the area and redirect his attention to something more positive, such as play or exercise.

### DIGGING TO KEEP COOL

Dogs often dig holes in the soil when they're outdoors and the weather is hot. The soil temperature just a few inches below the surface is considerably cooler, and the dog seeks to lower his body temperature by resting on cooler ground. The solution here is to provide a cooler place for the dog to rest, or to allow the animal to dig a cool resting place for himself.

## CAREFUL CORRECTION

The causes and cures of digging are straightforward, easily understood and easily managed. The most important thing to remember about a digging habit is that attempting to stop the dog from digging without replacing the behavior with a less annoying habit will create a neurosis in the dog. The neurotic behavior may very well be worse than the original problem of digging, so owners need to use caution when attempting to correct a digging problem.

### BOREDOM AND/OR FRUSTRATION

Boredom and frustration are probably the most common reasons for a dog to dig for what appears to be some unknown reason. Many dogs that are housed outdoors and tied to a

## CAUSE AND EFFECT

Frustration creates tension. Tension is often relieved by digging. Therefore, trying to stop the digging becomes pointless unless we examine the real cause of the digging and address its cure. That leads us back to the basic nature of the dog as a social creature that needs to live with a pack for his very survival.

or activities in which to participate with their owners. Toys and bones can definitely help alleviate boredom for short periods of time. However, the long-term picture suggests that a more permanent plan be instituted to prevent the urge to dig altogether. Supervised activity can solve the problem.

Installing a regular kennel run on a cement pad will stop the dog from digging. Many dogs live in kennels all their lives without developing neurotic behaviors, because their owners provide them with stimulation on a regular basis. Working a dog at hunting, obedience trialing, agility competition, tracking or another type of event, or even having the dog accompany you as you work around the property, are meaningful, healthy activities that give the dog a purpose in life so he never becomes frustrated. By the time he returns to his kennel at the end of his activity session, he is content to play with his toys by himself or just enjoy his dinner and rest.

long chain will dig due to lack of something to do. Dogs who run free in fenced-in yards often dig if they are not provided with interesting and appropriate stimuli. Sturdy toys to knock around and safe large bones on which to chew can keep dogs occupied for hours.

Dogs in the previous examples are often left for prolonged periods of time without human companionship

In dealing with a frustration problem in a dog that lives in the house, we usually see various forms of destructive behavior as the manifestation of the anxiety created by being separated from his human pack members. Digging in the carpet or cushions of upholstered furniture are just some of the manifestations.

Dogs are social creatures. When a dog owner goes to work and leaves his dog alone in the house for 8 to 10 hours a day, the dog begins to suffer from separation anxiety. Thus the stage is set for the frustration, tension and, ultimately, digging to emerge.

Crate training a dog is the ideal way to prevent separation anxiety and, at the same time, keep the dog and the house safe from destruction. The dog learns to see his crate as his own private den in which he feels safe and comfortable, despite the fact that he is separated from his pack members. A dog in the wild, for example, will seek out the safety of a hole in a sandy bank, in the base of an old tree or under the floor of a porch or wooden deck. There he will rest until he's ready to rejoin his pack. The same reaction occurs with the domestic dog. He needs a safe, comfortable place to stay while he's alone and while he awaits the return of his family (pack).

Just as the outdoor dog needs physical and mental stimulation, so does the indoor dog. Most dogs are not born to be couch potatoes. They need a purpose in order to live well-adjusted lives and be happy members of their home communities. An indoor dog who waits long hours during his owner's work day should be able

to look forward to some form of physical and mental activity when the owner returns.

If yours is a dog who spends all day indoors, alone, while you are at work, getting outdoors with the dog on weekends and days off is an excellent way to give the dog (and you!) healthy exercise. Playing games with the dog indoors during inclement weather and in the evenings when you are at home provides much-needed mental stimulation. Fetching games and teaching the dog to do tricks are excellent examples of indoor activities.

Keeping the dog busy and spending time with him when you are home, and providing a safe haven for him when you are not, will guarantee you a mentally and physically sound companion for many years to come. Best of all, your home and yard will be free of destruction caused by digging!

**Some dogs like to dig out a cozy niche for themselves, much as their ancestors used to do.**

# FEAR OF THUNDER AND OTHER NOISES

If you've ever seen a dog suffering from fear of the sounds of a thunderstorm, your heart had to go out to the animal. The dog shivers and shakes, crouches down as if he is trying to escape, hides in small, dark places and, in general, is unable to cope with normal life activities.

Many years ago I owned a lovely Standard Poodle named Jeannie. She was afraid of thunder and, the first moment she heard the sound of an approaching storm, she would run to the bathroom and hide in the tub. No amount of coaxing could bring her out until the storm passed and it was quiet again. Once the storm ended, she was fine and happy, ready to continue on with life as usual. This behavior lasted for

**You never know what might trigger a dog's fear, but many dogs hide to escape their imagined dangers.**

several years until one day when I met an old dog breeder who gave me an idea to help Jeannie.

I made a tape recording of a variety of sounds. It included the noises of a car motor racing, doors slamming, pots and pans being dropped on tile floors, bells ringing, car horns blowing, drum rolls that sounded like thunder, etc. I recorded enough sounds to make the tape last for about 10 minutes.

The man had told me, "Make happy, not havoc for the dog." I understood what he meant and set about the task of creating a happy atmosphere for Jeannie. I would find a way to replace her fear of thunder by creating a happy association with the very same sound. That thought immediately led me to food, since one of Jeannie's favorite things to do was eat!

After a short consultation with my breeder friend, I set up the training scheme to desensitize Jeannie to the sounds she feared. I couldn't stop the power of nature, but I could substitute her anxieties with pleasure. Here's how I did it:

Every day at feeding time, I set up the tape recorder on the kitchen counter. When I served her meal, I turned on the recording and set the volume at the lowest level. I let the recording play during the entire time she was eating. In other

**DOGGIE DESENSITIZATON**

Mealtime is the most popular time for desensitization training. However, some dogs are so besotted with retrieving that the owners can play the tapes while the dog participates in a game of fetch. Simply find a place and time when your dog naturally focuses on something he loves. During this time, introduce the sound recording at a barely audible level. Increase the volume during this "fun" time each day. Plan on using this desensitization training for at least a month so that the dog becomes acclimated to it and so makes a permanent association of happiness with the sounds.

words, I was beginning to create an association of the pleasures of mealtime with the sounds she feared.

Little by little, I increased the volume of the recording while Jeannie ate her meal. Being totally focused on her dinner, she ignored the sounds, which, over a period of several weeks, had grown quite loud.

After one month of using a gradual exposure to the worrisome sounds, Jeannie was no longer driven to jump into the tub when a storm arrived. She did, however, come running to me when she heard the noise of distant thunder. When that happened, she and I would go into the kitchen and I'd give her a dog biscuit and praise her for being so brave. Actually, I was teaching her that thunderstorms were good things that signaled a treat for her. They were no longer some invisible enemy to be feared, but merely a signal that promised something happy.

My wise old dog friend had given me good advice. And over the years, it has continued to prove effective for hundreds of my students who live with dogs afraid of various noises. Today, you can purchase tape recordings of sounds instead of making your own. Whether you make or buy a recording of sounds, be sure that you introduce it to the dog while he's occupied with a favorite activity.

**Urinating indoors can be a fear reaction.**

The treat jar can be an owner's (and a dog's) best friend when it comes to fear desensitization and rewarding for being such a brave dog!

BETTER DOG BEHAVIOR

# HOUSE-TRAINING AND URINE MARKING

Most dogs are trained to relieve themselves outdoors in designated areas. A few toy breeds are sometimes trained to relieve themselves indoors on newspaper or special "potty pads." Whatever type of dog you have and whatever method of house-training you've chosen for your dog, it's important that both you and the dog understand exactly where you want the dog to relieve himself. For sure, you don't want the dog to urinate or defecate wherever he is when the urge hits him.

Dogs by nature are clean animals. Unless provided with no other option, they do not relieve themselves near the sources of their food or places where they rest and sleep. Humans have the same instincts of cleanliness and order. That natural trait is one of the reasons why dogs make ideal companions to mankind.

House-training means teaching a dog to use a predetermined specified area in which to relieve himself whenever he feels the need to urinate or defecate. Urine marking is an entirely

different matter. Dogs, particularly unneutered males, mark their territory with urine in order to inform other dogs of their presence.

When there is a female in season in the neighborhood, male dogs will keep busy marking every available upright object as a warning to other prospective suitors to stay away from her. Intact males have been known to escape from their own homes and spend the female's entire estrus period outside her home, marking every bush, tree and lamp post! Since females are in season for about 21 days, twice a year, this becomes a real nuisance to the owners of both the female in question and the marking males, to say nothing of the possibility of an unwanted pregnancy.

The obvious solution to this problem is simple: spay the female and neuter the male. Once hormone production ceases, the dogs will settle down and become easier to live with, more devoted to their families and homes. Just the thought of unwanted puppies is enough to make altering your pet worthwhile.

## HOW TO HOUSE-TRAIN

First, you will need a crate for your dog. For the adult dog, the crate should be wide and long enough so the dog can lie down with his legs outstretched, and tall enough so he can stand up without rubbing his head on the top of the crate. If you have a puppy, you'll need to purchase a crate that will fit the dog when he becomes an adult. The pet shop salesperson will help you choose the size that will fit your puppy when he reaches maturity, based on the dog's breed.

   If the puppy is very small and his projected mature size is very large, then you should block off the back portion of the crate so that he has use of a smaller area of the crate, suitable for him at his

### HOUSE-TRAINING SUCCESS

House-training your dog should begin the day you bring the puppy home. In the case of an adult dog that is not well trained, you can begin all over again just as if you had acquired the dog today. Either way, the method is the same and the process will take time, but you will achieve your goal if you use a proven method rather than harsh corrections every time the dog makes a mistake in the house.

current age and size. Remember that if he has too much room in the crate, he may use one section of it for a relief area and the other for sleeping and resting. That would teach him to relieve himself inside his crate, thus creating what is known as a "dirty dog." By

Any upright object can be a target for a male dog's urine-marking.

PHOTO BY PAULETTE BRAUN.

## WHAT KIND OF CRATE?

The basic types of crates are wire, fiberglass and fabric mesh. You may want to discuss your choice with the breeder from whom you purchased your dog or the pet-shop clerk. With wire and fabric crates, the dog can see out on all sides; these are good for use in the home, although fabric-mesh crates are not recommended for chewers and/or diggers. With a fiberglass crate, only the door will provide a view for the dog as the bottom, top and sides of the crate are solid fiberglass. These are best used as carriers and travel crates.

providing just the right amount of space for him to be comfortable, he will quickly learn to satisfy his urine and bowel urges outside his crate so that his bed and resting area remains clean and dry.

Puppies under the age of six months do not have full control of their bladder muscles, so taking them outdoors often during the day is essential. Adult dogs have full bladder control, so they can remain in their crates for longer periods of time. All dogs usually need to relieve themselves after play periods, after each meal and after waking from naps. All dogs also should be taken outdoors just before their owners retire at night. Most dogs, including puppies, can "hold it" through the night, though the little ones will usually wake their owners by 4 or 5 a.m. to go out. Grown dogs will usually sleep until they hear the family stirring in the morning.

When I'm house-training a puppy, I always take him out whenever he indicates by whining or acting restlessly that he has "to go." He will usually have to urinate and only occasionally have to defecate during the night. When he's done, I bring him back inside and put him in his crate again without making a fuss over him. I don't want him to get so excited that he can't go back to sleep for a few more hours. (Getting up for the day at 4 a.m. just isn't on my agenda!)

Place the crate in the family room or wherever the family spends most of its time. Since dogs are social creatures, they need to be near their pack members (you!) and not stuck away in some isolated place such as the laundry room or garage. If you have a big kitchen and spend a lot of time there, put the crate in a corner of the room where the dog can see and hear you as you go about your activities.

Use a clean towel to line the bottom of the crate, and give the dog only one toy in the crate. During the house-training process, do not put food or water in the crate. Eating and drinking will activate your dog's digestive processes, which will ultimately

Baby gates are useful tools for partitioning off rooms in the home to keep your dog in safe, dog-proof areas.

### CRATE LINING
Never line your dog's crate with newspaper. Most puppies are raised from birth on newspaper, thus making them think that the newspaper is a relief area. Soft cushions, down-filled comforters, etc., do not make appropriate bedding for dogs. They are soft and very chewable, so only the older, more mature dog should be offered this type of bedding. Puppies see soft, fluffy things as items to be chewed and torn apart. Towels are the ideal material for bedding because terrycloth can be washed and dried whenever necessary and it can be replaced whenever it suffers the ravages of teething puppies.

defeat your purpose in training as well as make the dog very uncomfortable as he tries to "hold it."

Whenever you take the dog outdoors, always take him to the predetermined area that you have chosen as his relief area. Be consistent about it. Have him on his collar and lead, go directly to the relief area and wait there with him for no more than five minutes. If he voids, praise him and bring him into the house. He should then be given time to play in whatever room you're using at the time. Do not allow him to wander unsupervised throughout the house. Controlling him at all times during the house-training process will be the key to success.

If he did not relieve himself when the two of you were outdoors, put him back in his crate and wait for 30 minutes. Then ask him again if he wants to go "Hurry up" (or whatever command words you've chosen to indicate going out). Take him back to his relief area and wait with him for another five minutes. When he voids, praise him and bring him back into the house for some playtime.

**STEPS FOR CRATE-TRAINING**
Following is a schedule of steps for crate-training a dog. Follow each step in order, and don't skip any steps, so that the dog gradually becomes accustomed to his crate. Soon he'll learn to love his special area and the security it represents; plus, he'll have learned where and when to eliminate.

1. Tell the dog, "It's crate time!" and place him in the crate with a small treat (a piece of cheese or a biscuit). Let him stay in the crate for five minutes while you are in the room with him. Do not talk to the dog, but do let him see you as you move around or simply sit and read, write or watch television. After five minutes, release the dog from the crate and praise him lavishly. Never let him out when he's making a fuss; rather, wait until he is quiet before releasing him from the crate.

2. Repeat Step 1 several times the first day.

3. The next day, place the dog in the crate as described in Step 1, but this time let him stay there for ten minutes. Do this several times and notice how the dog is becoming accustomed to staying in his crate without being stressed. Always praise the dog when you release him from his crate.

4. Continue building time in 5-minute increments until the dog will stay in his crate for 30 minutes with you in the room. Remember that after prolonged stays in his crate, you should take him out to relieve himself as soon as you release him.

5. Now you'll start at the beginning again. This time, you will accustom the dog to the crate without you in the room with him. Let the dog stay in his crate for five minutes while you are out of the room. Praise lavishly when you release him.

6. Once again, build crate time in five-minute increments, but with you out of the room. When the dog will stay willingly in his crate for 30 minutes with you out of the room (he may even fall asleep), he'll be ready to stay in it for several hours at a time when you must leave him alone. (There are millions of families who go to work, school, etc., each day and leave their dogs in crates to avoid damage to their belongings and, most importantly, to protect their dogs from harm.)

The basis of house-training is that the dog will use his acute sense of smell to locate the proper relief site. Dogs with fenced yards learn quickly to go to their spots on their own.

Once you have a crate-trained dog, you may notice that he occasionally goes into his crate on his own, just to nap or chew on a bone. At times when your house is filled with guests, he'll likely greet everyone as they arrive but soon wander off to the peace and security of his own special place. That tells you that he really loves his private space!

Being consistent, taking the dog out frequently, giving lots of praise, exercising control and providing supervision are the elements necessary for house-training any dog, puppy or adult. If you follow the procedures as described, soon you and your dog will be ready to enjoy a full, rewarding and clean life together.

## URINE MARKING

The passing of urine for the purpose of marking a territory does not occur before the age of six months. Dogs can be motivated to urine-mark as a result of the approach or appearance of another dog, a threat to their personal territory, the presence of a female dog in season or the need to identify their own pack members (in this case, you!).

Male dogs that have not been neutered are much more prone to micturate than neutered individuals, simply due to the presence of testosterone. Any dog that urine-marks away from his own territory is broadening his territory by sending out a signal that says, "This is now my territory and I'm putting my mark on it to prove it." In addition, males will mark whenever they detect females in season. In other words, some dogs will mark whenever and wherever they feel the need; thus, restricting where the dog goes helps to restrict marking.

A dog can easily be trained not to urine-mark. Keep the dog on lead and keep him away from

It doesn't take dogs long to learn the routine of going out—and coming back in!

Your dog may appreciate a cozy bed in addition to his crate, giving him an extra place to cuddle up. However, it's best to wait until the dog is house-trained, when he's less likely to have an accident in the bed.

upright objects such as doorways, tables, chairs, etc. When you go near any standing object and the dog sniffs it in preparation for lifting his leg, tell him "No, leave it!" in an authoritative tone of voice. Quickly move away from the object and tell him he's a good boy.

Wait a few minutes and once again move toward the object of his interest. When he begins sniffing again, repeat the command "Leave it" and move away. Praise him again and repeat this process until he accepts the fact that marking is unacceptable behavior. He will soon learn that emptying his bladder for relief and urine-marking are two different behaviors. The first is acceptable and pleases you; the second is unacceptable and produces a stern correction from you.

The most important element in training your dog not to mark is your ability and willingness to pay constant attention to the dog when he's in a place or position of marking. An owner who looks away and ignores the dog will not notice how often the dog lifts his leg as they stroll along. Thus the dog learns that leg-lifting is OK, and he'll urine-mark wherever and whenever instinct tells him to do it. A few months of diligently monitoring the dog will pay big dividends in a dog that possesses good manners wherever he goes.

Responsibility falls on dog owners to channel their dogs' energy into proper and constructive activities. Obedience training is a challenging venue that dogs and owners can enjoy together.

# INAPPROPRIATE PLAY BEHAVIOR

*The puppy was growing bigger every day. Soon he'd weigh 70 or 80 pounds and he'd be as tall as the family's little boy. He was a good dog, obedient, happy, eager to please and very friendly toward everyone. He especially enjoyed playing rough games with the owner, a big man who also loved the tugging games.*

*However, when the little boy played with him, the puppy would grab the child's arm and begin pulling him as if he were a rag doll. Usually the cries of the child would be enough to make the dog stop using his mouth. But the owner realized that the problem was getting worse and he would have to do something. He wasn't sure what to do, but he knew that the dog's rough behavior was becoming dangerous to the child.*

## ROUGH PLAY

By teaching the dog to use his mouth to grab and hold things, the dog's chase and kill instincts are heightened, and he confuses these instincts with play behaviors. That's when the owners realize that they have a major problem on their hands.

They love the dog and enjoy interacting with him, yet they don't want the growling, grabbing, pulling and tugging behaviors acted out on them.

Ideally the puppy owner will realize, perhaps with the help of a puppy class, that the humans in the puppy's life can and should teach the puppy proper play behaviors that will be safe and fun throughout the dog's life. If this has not happened and the puppy is already beginning to enjoy overly rough play, then the owner must retrain the dog so that he learns how to play gently.

For example, never play tug-of-war with a dog. When he puts something in his mouth that you are holding, let go of the item. Don't hold on to it, because that will invite the dog to pull. Any resistance from you will cause the dog to resist in kind. That resistance initiates a tug-of-war game. The tug-of-war game teaches the dog to grab and hold.

Instead, teach the dog how to retrieve and carry things for you. Have him learn to fetch his toys and bring them back to you so you can throw them again. Give him

## LEARNED BEHAVIOR

Inappropriate play behavior is usually learned rather than inherited. Playing rough games with a puppy teaches the puppy to treat all humans roughly. As the puppy matures, the dog's strength and size usually become too much for his owners to handle. In addition, the rough behavior, which began as play, frequently turns into a serious form of aggression.

small items to carry as he goes with you from room to room in your home or from the house to your car. Many dogs learn to bring in the morning newspaper. Others fetch their leads for their owners before going for walks. All of these behaviors are fun for the dog and give him a feeling of purpose and importance.

## NUISANCE BARKING

Many owners make the mistake of teaching their puppies to bark. Since young puppies don't bark overly loudly, owners worry that their dog won't bark when he grows up, so they teach him to bark. Then, when the dog matures, he thinks that barking is a great pastime and his noisy behavior soon becomes a neighborhood nuisance.

It isn't necessary to teach a puppy to bark. When the dog matures, a well-adjusted, sound-minded dog will bark at all the right times for all the right reasons. The owner doesn't have to do

Tug-of-war games with a puppy can lead to problems as the dog matures, such as aggression, possessiveness with toys and uncontrollable behavior during play.

anything to train the dog when and where to bark. The dog's instinct will tell him when to bark. Furthermore, if the owner has built a strong bond with his dog from the time the dog was young, the grown dog will express his feelings and concerns by barking.

For example, the adult dog will bark to warn of strange noises and things (including strange people) in his territory. He'll bark to get his owner's attention for something he wants. Maybe it's time to eat and he's hungry. Maybe it's time to go out to relieve himself. Perhaps he's excited when he sees his owner preparing to take him for a ride in the car, which is one of his favorite things to do. He'll bark to invite another dog or cat to play. He'll even bark to ask one of his human pack members to play with him. A dog should not be discouraged from this means of communication.

## CHASING GAMES

Children often teach the dog to "play-chase" without realizing what the eventual results will be. If you call the dog to you and then proceed to chase him around the room or yard, he will misinterpret this as a game of "catch me if you can." Be assured that even a young puppy can run faster than most people can, so there is little hope of your being successful in catching him!

When children chase the puppy, he joins in the fun even more enthusiastically due to the squealing and yelling that the children add to the game. Before long, every time the puppy hears his name being called, he launches into an exciting game destined to wear out the hardiest of kids or adults. In other words, the dog wins and the people become annoyed, even angry, at the dog when they cannot catch him. It's really a no-win situation for all.

The bottom line here is: never chase the dog and don't allow children to chase the dog. If you want the dog to come to you, stand or sit still and, using a happy, gentle tone of voice, encourage the dog to come and receive a treat and praise. When shown the correct way to call a dog, children love to sit on the ground and coax the dog to them. The treat and affection that results proves to be a positive experience for both!

**Appropriate play behavior is learned through interactions with littermates. These Clumber Spaniel siblings are learning the ropes with a little friendly roughhousing.**

The protective instincts of guard-dog breeds can be enhanced in a positive manner through specialized training.

Grabbing forbidden objects can be annoying to you and dangerous to the pup. Puppies can't tell which things around the house can cause them harm, so you must keep off-limits items away from your curious puppy.

lying on the floor. The puppy sees an item on the floor. He goes to investigate it and realizes it smells like one of his pack—you or someone else in the family. He grabs the item and someone sees him, and the chase begins. Very quickly, the puppy learns that picking up dropped items will get someone's attention, so he repeats the behavior as often as possible.

The first and most obvious solution is never to let things end up on the floor. If there's nothing to grab and run away with, the dog won't be able to do it. Teach children to put away their clothes and shoes in designated places and never leave them out as an invitation to the dog.

If the puppy does get hold of some item, see if you can get

### GRABBING FORBIDDEN ITEMS

Once again, children are usually the creators of this undesirable behavior, which the dog perceives as play and the humans perceive as unacceptable. Most times this situation is created by a curious puppy and small children who leave items of clothing and shoes

him to come to you by sitting down on a chair or even the floor and calling the dog in a cajoling tone of voice. When he comes to you, say "Out" or "Give" and take the item from him. Then praise immediately and replace the forbidden item with one of the dog's own toys. It is better, though, to prevent this unwanted behavior rather than correct it.

In addition, provide plenty of stimulating toys to interest your dog and keep him busy so he won't even get the idea to grab inappropriate items in the first place. Remember that boredom

and lack of exercise and activities are usually the causes for many unwanted behaviors. Also keep in mind that some breeds of dog are more prone to grabbing and chewing things than others. The retrievers and sporting dogs love to carry things in their mouths. Poodles love to chew soft items. Some of the large working dogs like nothing better than to chew and gnaw on hard objects such as bones, wood, furniture legs and the like.

One final note here: whenever I have a dog that loves to grab things and chew them, I experiment with his toys and find something he really loves. Then, when I see him looking as if he's bored or contemplating some behavior I don't want, I excitedly coax him to retrieve his beloved toy and carry it around. I usually say something like, "Get your pretty! Oh how pretty you look with that toy! That's a pretty toy!"

*Some very creative (and very trusting) owners find truly unique ways to keep their dogs active!*

## FAVORITE TOY

I teach this trick to my classes, too, and I have had many Labrador Retrievers and Golden Retrievers who love to carry a favorite toy around when they go for walks. You remember the Golden whom I mentioned previously, had a favorite cotton gardening glove that he carried in his mouth wherever he went for years.

# JUMPING

Dogs jump for all sorts of reasons. They jump on people, on furniture, on forbidden objects. They jump over fences and barriers. They jump when they get excited and often when they're extremely happy.

Most owners don't particularly mind if their dog jumps under certain circumstances, but they do mind in other situations. For example, a dog that jumps up on the sofa may be breaking the house rules, but when he jumps over some fallen log in the back yard, he's well within his limits.

On the other hand, some owners have no objection to their dogs' jumping on beds and furniture, but do not want them to jump on people. Some owners train their dogs in sporting events, such as obedience training, in which jumping is a major component. Those same owners, however, teach their dogs not to jump over fences in their yards.

Let's break down this matter of jumping to examine the reasons that dogs jump and some of the things you can do if you want to teach your dog not to jump in some of those situations. As with most behaviors, we can solve behavior problems once we identify the causes.

## TYPES OF JUMPING BEHAVIORS

### JUMPING UP ON OWNER AND FAMILY MEMBERS

The dog jumps up on you, the owner, and other family members for recognition and affection. It's simply his way of saying, "Hey, I'm here! I want to say hello and have you give me some attention." Negative reactions on your part will only cause more problems in the dog, so you must find a way to meet the dog's needs without having him jump up on you. This can be accomplished by having the dog sit for attention. In addition, if the dog is sitting, you must get down to the dog's level; thus, he doesn't feel the need to jump up in your face. With a small dog, this means bending down low. Extend your hands down to his shoulders as you pet him, and smile as you look into his face. Tell him to sit and, when he does, praise him for being such a good dog.

Now's the time to teach "Off!" This young Chessie is only knee-high now but will grow to be much taller and heavier, and capable of knocking someone down if he jumps up.

If he still insists on jumping up, turn and walk away from him. Ignore him and do not give him the opportunity to jump on you again. When you're ready, turn to face him and give him a firm command to sit, at which point you will bend down once more, with your hands petting him and your face close to him. Softly praise him as you hold him in the sit position and tell him he's being good. This excitable type of dog needs soft voices and slow, deliberate handling to get him to settle down and maintain a sit position as he receives your attention and affection.

While owners may enjoy hugs from their own pets, will their guests feel the same way about such an enthusiastic greeting?

In the case of the large dog, if he's an excitable individual, put him on his collar and lead before you try to get control with the sit command. This will give you the ability to get physical control of the dog before you begin to teach him how to sit calmly whenever he wants your attention.

If the dog complies with your sit command without acting wildly, praise him, pet him, even give him a biscuit as a reward for his polite behavior. As with the excitable dogs, calmer dogs should also be given plenty of attention once they settle down. At that time they, too, should receive a treat.

It won't be long before your dog begins to get the message that sitting politely in front of you or other family members will produce positive attention and a food reward. The food treat should be used for some time and then slowly weaned away, just leaving the praise and attention for which he's asking. Any form of negative reaction from you when he asks for attention and affection will result in more undesirable behavior, perhaps more serious problem behavior, that may prove difficult to correct. Thus, keeping the lessons positive will bring desired results.

### JUMPING UP ON GUESTS

Again, dogs jump on guests in the home because they want to greet the people and get attention. (Did you ever think that your dog thinks guests have come to see him, not you?) They also jump because they're curious and are attempting to discover who this new person is.

The solution is much the same as it was for jumping on family members. You're still going to have to control the dog, as most guests are not prepared to help you train your dog. Some are even reluctant to work with dogs in general. Therefore, you should put the dog on his collar and lead before you go to the door to admit the guest.

Have a biscuit in your pocket and take the dog to the door. Have the dog sit beside you as you call out to the guest to enter. The dog

will probably try to pop up when he sees the guest walk through the doorway. At this point, be firm and insist that the dog sit calmly beside you. The first few times you try this, it will be difficult to control the dog, but you must get him to obey before you can reward him.

Once the dog is sitting next to you, no matter how reluctantly, give the biscuit to your guest and ask him to give it to your dog as you explain to him what you're

This photogenic German Shepherd jumps up to strike a handsome pose.

"Whatcha got there?" Some dogs are very curious and won't be satisfied until they get the chance to investigate. Holding the object out of his reach only further piques his interest.

training the dog to do. Have the guest tell the dog he's a good boy as he gives him the treat.

Next, invite your guest to come and sit down for a chat. Keep the dog on lead and have him stay quietly beside you as you visit with your friend. Another biscuit and more praise from your guest when the visit is over will reinforce your lesson.

If the visit with your friend is planned for a longer period than just a few minutes, wait until the dog settles down and becomes accustomed to having the guest in the house before you release him. Most dogs settle down quickly with visitors and treat them like family members once they observe your friendliness toward the guest.

You may be surprised to find that after a few weeks of this controlled greeting training, your dog will race to the door whenever he hears the doorbell ring. He'll sit automatically and look back to make sure that you're coming to answer the bell. It will be obvious that the dog is excited about the arrival of a guest because he thinks the person is coming to see him and bringing him a treat. He'll never guess that the person is there to visit with you! No matter what the dog thinks, having him under control at the arrival of visitors will be a pleasure for you and most impressive to your friends.

With a large and heavy dog, it is helpful if he can use his jumping skills to get into the car on his own.

**Why do dogs jump up on each other? It's just plain fun!**

### INVESTIGATIVE JUMPING

Oftentimes a dog jumps up on his owner to investigate something that the owner is holding in his hands. This is a manifestation of the dog's natural sense of curiosity. By understanding that the dog is intelligent and very sensitive to his environment, we can cure this problem easily.

If the object that you are holding is not dangerous, let the dog investigate it by sight and smell. Don't try to hold it up out of his reach. Simply lower the object so he can study it at close range. If the object is dangerous, tell the dog "No" and turn away from him if he tries to jump on you. If he continues to try to reach the article, have him sit and then begin to divert his attention onto something he knows and enjoys. "Where's your ball? Go get your ball!" is a good diversion. Quickly remove the dangerous article from the dog's presence and concentrate on keeping him occupied with alternative behaviors.

### JUMPING FOR HIS FOOD

Many owners allow their dogs to jump up at kitchen counters or even on themselves while they are preparing the dogs' food. This is unnecessary and can even be dangerous if the dog knocks a person over or causes the owner to spill something or drop something breakable.

Again, this habit can be corrected by having the dog sit and stay while his food is being prepared. If you are alone and have no way to enforce the sit/stay command while you prepare the dog's food, simply put the dog on his collar and lead and tie him to a doorknob or some sturdy object.

Once the food is prepared, place the bowl on the floor and release the dog by saying "OK, good boy." If a family member is holding the dog's lead while you are preparing the dog's food, have the person release the dog after you've placed the bowl in the spot where you normally feed the dog.

### HORMONAL JUMPING

Females that have not been spayed and males that have not been neutered often exhibit unwanted behaviors toward family members. These behaviors are all part of the dog's sexual

A treat is best given with the dog on all fours. This may take a little practice, because most dogs just can't wait for their reward.

## COMFY CHAIR

Some owners even designate special resting places for their dogs on certain pieces of furniture. This way, an owner preserves other pieces of furniture from unwanted dog hair while allowing the dog to enjoy his own special furniture. Usually an old sheet or blanket draped over the dog's furniture will teach the dog where his personal spot awaits him. Regardless, every dog needs a place where he can rest and feel comfortable while he's among his pack members. Wicker baskets, oversized stuffed pillows and dog beds are all available for purchase and prove to be favorites with dogs.

they find around the house. Large dogs frequently grab their owners' legs and ride them as they hold on with their front paws. If there are small children in the house, dogs (of any size) may try to ride them as they play on the floor. They also lift their legs on the furniture in the house as their way of marking their territory.

The owner should talk with his veterinarian about spaying or neutering. Both are simple procedures that are not prohibitively expensive, and they cause the animal only minimal discomfort. The whole procedure and stay at the vet's clinic usually lasts no more than 24 to 36 hours. The doctor will remove a few stitches after 10 to 14 days.

In addition to removing the dog's sexual drives and breeding capability, altering the dog makes him or her a better, more devoted-to-home-and-family pet. The dog loses the urge to wander, to seek out the company of other dogs and to act overly protective of his owners and home. On the other hand, the dog remains a fine watchdog around the house.

### JUMPING ON FURNITURE AND OTHER OBJECTS

Some breeds are more prone to jumping up on furniture than others. They spring from one chair to the next like little mountain goats seeking higher ground. Large dogs jump onto

drive and serve as practice for breeding or as an outlet for hormonal urges brought on by females in estrus.

Small dogs often ride their owners' feet and ankles. They will ride pillows or other soft objects

sofas and settle in for cozy naps while their owners wonder how to train them to stay on the floor. Even the breeds that don't jump, Corgis, Dachshunds, Basset Hounds, for example, love to find soft, elevated resting places like beds and furniture.

If the owner doesn't want the dog on the furniture, the dog must be removed from the area whenever the owner cannot be there to supervise the dog. One successful way of teaching the dog not to jump up onto furniture is to use little wooden mousetraps.

Purchase some new mouse-traps and set them, without using food as bait. Place them on the furniture cushion and cover them with a light dishtowel. This will allow the traps to go off when the dog touches them, yet he won't get his feet caught in them, because the towel will protect him. The loud snap of the traps going off will alarm the dog and cause him to get down off the furniture.

You, the owner, should be nearby when this takes place. When you hear the sound of popping traps, go into the room and offer solace to the dog with "You poor boy. Did that sofa try to bite you? Well, you stay here on the floor with me, good boy."

Covered mousetraps are an easy way to teach large dogs to stay off furniture. With small

> **WINDOW TO THE WORLD**
> A dog learns that an upholstered chair in front of a window is an ideal place to perch while he watches life go on outside. This problem can be corrected by moving the chair so the dog cannot see out the window. In other words, by removing the temptation, we remove the problem.

dogs, this will take a little more planning, but you can teach them to stay off furniture, too.

Let's say the dog loves to jump up on the sofa. Take a collection of metal pots and pans, pan lids,

*Just watch your dog jump for joy when there's food to be had.*

phone directories, unopened food cans, metal utensils like cooking spoons and spatulas (not knives or forks) and anything else that rattles and covers the surface of the sofa cushions. Next, leave the room and listen for the sound of your dog hopping around on the sofa, trying to get comfortable amid the clatter and clutter.

He will soon learn that there just isn't a spot in which to get comfortable, so he'll jump back down onto the floor. At that point, you rush into the room and praise him for being on the floor with "Good boy! You're on the floor! What a good boy you are!"

Both the mousetraps for large breeds and the clutter for small breeds are harmless, effective ways to teach dogs to stay off

*What a performance! A willing dog will literally jump through hoops for the owner he loves.*

furniture. You don't need to be negative about it and cause the dog to develop new undesirable behaviors. Just emphasize the good behavior and ignore that which you don't want.

### JUMPING OVER FENCES/BARRIERS
To get out of an enclosure, to run free, to join other dogs or people, to go after an antagonist such as a child who teases the dog or a strange dog who threatens the dog's house or yard, to chase a

cat, to run after a child on a bicycle—these are all reasons for some dogs' jumping. A dog that jumps over a baby gate in the house, for example, is probably doing it to join you in another room. Instead of leaving the dog in one room while you go to another, take the dog with you. He just wants to be close to you, his pack leader. Common sense tells us that, in many of these

**Whether you use a fence or an exercise pen, you must be sure that your dog's area of confinement is secure and escape-proof.**

Here's a clever stunt. Don't underestimate your dog's ability to figure out how to climb up, jump over, squeeze under, etc.

no longer perceives the child as a threat, he will stop trying to jump the fence and chase the child. For further details, see the chapter on chasing.

Some dogs jump fences and barriers because they simply want to run free. It's difficult at best to train a dog with a strong drive for freedom to control himself and stay within a closed area such as the home or yard. These dogs are usually hyperactive, nervous individuals who possess little or no self-confidence. They are frequently referred to as "escape artists." Scolding and/or punishment are not recommended for these dogs, as the problem will usually escalate as a result. Professional

situations, we can solve the problem by simply removing the temptation for the dog to jump.

If a dog attempts to jump the fence in his back yard to chase a child who is teasing him, the solution must be applied to the child, not the dog. Once the dog

### CONTROLLED JUMPING

Finally, teaching the dog when and where to jump correctly will satisfy the dog's urge to jump. It's easy to devise a low jump out of two bricks and an old broom handle. The dog will not concern himself with the height of the jump, but he will get excited about the jumping activity itself. Many behaviorists feel that "To teach a dog not to jump the fence, teach him to jump on command. Then he'll only jump when you tell him to!" That proves true in most cases. Most dogs love to jump. They just need to be shown where and when to turn a nuisance behavior into a fun activity.

help is usually indicated in these cases. The dog's veterinarian can direct the owner to a behavioral consultant who is trained to effectively address the problem. For further details, see the chapter on running away.

Sometimes a dog finds himself in an enclosed yard and isolated from his pack when his owner cannot be there to supervise him in the house. Being alone often leads to feelings of insecurity and anxiety. This condition is known as isolation frustration. In response to this, he jumps the fence to seek out his pack members. This condition can be prevented by a series of controlled activities.

Allowing adequate time each day to interact with the dog in meaningful activities will help to provide enough stimulation for the dog so that, when he is alone, he will be content to rest quietly in his crate. Obedience training, agility training, long leisurely walks, sessions of playing fetch or other physically demanding games, periods of soothing grooming and rides in the car are all things that your dog will enjoy doing with you. In addition, the dog needs to be trained in basic manners so that he develops self-confidence. Remember that your praise and enthusiasm in all endeavors will make the whole matter successful.

Is your dog a natural jumper? Teaching him to conquer a series of low hurdles is fun and challenging for both of you.

# RUNNING AWAY

*The little dog was a very sociable creature. He loved people, especially little people. He also loved other dogs and cats. He would often hear the neighborhood children playing in the street in front of his house, and he yearned to join them. Sometimes his owner would open the front door to greet the postman or a delivery person. The little dog would use the opportunity to dash out the door and race down the path to join the children at play.*

*This behavior made his owner furious, and the man would come running after the little dog. Eventually he'd catch him and, when he did, he would pick up the dog and scold him. The little dog did not like it when his owner yelled at him, so each time he dashed into the street to play, he would run faster so his owner couldn't catch him.*

*This behavior, in turn, made the owner more furious and eventually it became an ugly ritual of the dog's running, the owner's catching him, the dog's being punished, the dog's beginning to dislike his owner, the owner's beginning to dislike the dog. In other words, it became a no-win situation that would eventually end in the owner's getting rid of the little dog.*

Running out of the house, dashing out of the car when the door opens, finding a way to escape from a fenced yard, breaking free from his collar and lead when out for a walk: these are all behaviors that cause owners a great deal of distress, and oftentimes they lead to serious trouble for dogs, even to fatal accidents if the animal is hit by a car. Once again, it's important to understand why the dog runs away before attempting to correct the problem.

One thing is certain: a great deal of understanding and patience will be necessary in order to correct the situation. Further, it will take time to alter the dog's bad habit if he's been running away for some time. Actually, it can take six to eight weeks before the dog will reliably stay at home.

I like to address the problem of running away by concentrating on positive things to teach the dog rather than on correcting the problem. Time and energy spent on trying to correct the dog's habit is wasted time and energy as far as I'm concerned. I'd much rather replace the bad behavior with something desirable and rewarding for both the dog and the owner. After all, everyone enjoys a celebration, while nobody likes correction.

The method I use with all dogs that come to me for training, puppies and adults alike, is simple and easy to implement. First, I explain that I never use the word "Come" when teaching a dog to come to me. The sound of the word can be overly authoritative and so harsh that dogs are often motivated to run away rather than come to the caller.

Usually, when a person calls a dog to come, the person is in a hurry to get the dog to respond, frightened that the dog will run into the road and be hit by a car or otherwise nervous or anxious. Therefore, the tone of voice that the person uses is not conducive to having the dog respond in a favorable manner. The dog hears that harsh, frantic tone of voice and reacts fearfully to it. Thus, the person has created a reverse response to his command rather than the response he seeks.

Instead of setting up the dog for failure, I create a happy, positive atmosphere in which the dog will be eager to respond to the caller. How? By teaching the dog to answer a question.

## HAVE A "BICKY"

I use the word "bicky" for all food treats, and the dog relates the word to special food rewards. I use pieces of cut-up chicken, pieces of cut-up sausage, little chunks of cheddar cheese and other soft foods. I never use dry dog biscuits, because I want the dog to receive instant gratification rather than having to take the time to chew up the treat before he realizes he's being rewarded.

Yes, you read the previous sentence correctly! I ask the dog a question. Here's how it works. I teach dogs and owners how to play the "Where are you?" game. It's fun, fast and guaranteed to get

## WHERE DID YOU GO?

Chances are, when the dog is called back to the person he started with, he will run to the original room where they began. Not finding the person there, he will then have to listen to the sound of the person's voice to locate him—be ready for an enthusiastic greeting when he does.

saying a word to the dog, the people should go into two different rooms in the house to await their turns to play.

Now the dog, knowing that the people have treats, will follow one of the people. Thus, the other person begins the game. When ready, the person without the dog starts calling excitedly to the dog by saying things like, "Fido, where are you? Come get a bicky. I've got a bicky! Where are you? See if you can find me. I've got a bicky for you. Where are you?"

It's important to pay special attention to the way you call the dog and the amount of calling you do. First, your voice must be happy and excited, eliciting curiosity about the "bicky" while emphasizing the "Where are you?" part. Next, you must keep up a constant flow of conversation to the dog until the dog finds you.

Remember that the dog has no idea where the caller is located in the house. All he hears is the person's voice. Therefore, the calling must be a steady stream of happy talk that will excite the dog and make him search for the person.

When the dog finds the person, a major celebration begins. First, the dog gets the promised "bicky." The dog also receives a big hug and lots of praise and hand-clapping from the

the correct response from the dog without your ever uttering that dreaded command "Come."

Begin by playing the game indoors with the dog not wearing his collar and lead. Have two family members each take three or four pieces of delicious food treats in their hands. Next, without

Ah, the joy of a good, uninhibited run! All dogs need free time off leash to stretch their legs and scamper at will (in a secure area, of course!).

person. We want the dog to realize that he won the game of hide-and-seek and that he's a real hero in our eyes.

While the dog is celebrating his success at finding the person, the person whom he followed initially leaves the first room and goes to hide in another room. Now the dog will have to search for that person, too. As soon as the celebration with the first person he found is over, that person calls out "It's your turn" to the other person. Now the process of calling and finding begins all over again. Pretty soon the dog gets the idea that he must listen carefully and follow the sound of the caller in order to get a treat and a celebration. In other words, the dog soon learns that going to the caller is a wonderful,

rewarding experience and that he always wins the game!

Once secure in the rules of the game, you can take the dog outdoors to a secure fenced area and show the dog that he can play the "Where are you?" game outdoors, too. Hiding behind a tree, ducking down beneath a bench or behind a trash can and popping around the corner of a house are all possible ways for owners to hide. Just be sure to vary your hiding place so the dog is challenged by the game.

This game is particularly enjoyable for children and dogs to play together. Kids can get into the tiniest places such as a corner of the shower, under a table, behind a sofa or in a closet. Dogs love searching in new and different places and receiving

## THE KEY TO "COME"

Without ever commanding the dog to "Come," the owner gets the dog to respond instantly, providing that he uses that happy "let's play the game" tone of voice. That's the key to success in the "Where are you?" game. Keep your voice happy, fast-paced and excited. Make that dog want more than anything to get to you in a hurry to celebrate and possibly even get a treat. Make his coming to you happy and positive every time—even surprise him with an extra-special morsel now and then.

proven successful in getting the dog to come when you want him about 99% of the time. Dogs stop chasing cats and come flying to their owners. They leave their doggie friends and come racing home when they hear the question "Where are you?" They turn on a dime and sprint across the yard just to get in on a celebration with their owners.

Try it. You and your dog will like it, and your problem will be over. Now, while teaching a dog to come when he's called is a significant half of solving the running-away problem, the other half is just as important. A dog must also learn not to run away when the front door is open or when he's in the car and you open the car door.

The solution? Teach the dog to "Stay." This is a basic beginner exercise taught in every dog obedience class. Once taught, it gives the owner control of the dog without having to keep him tied up all the time, and it's easy to teach. Let me tell you how.

First, put the dog on collar and lead. Have a few tasty treats in your right hand and the lead in your left hand. Have the dog sit beside you on your left side. Place your food hand at the dog's nose and say "Stay." Immediately pivot out in front of the dog and stay up close to him, toe to toe. Keep the food hand still and let the dog nibble the treats, but

rewards from their young friends. Just be sure, when teaching children how to play this game, that they understand the importance of a big celebration each time the dog finds them.

I have taught this game to thousands of dogs and owners, and I can tell you that it has

be sure to save a good-sized piece for the final step with praise.

At first, just count to five and then return to stand beside the dog as you were at the start. Give the final treat to the dog when you get back to him and praise lavishly as you do. Over the next two weeks, build the stay part of the exercise up to a count of 30 seconds with you standing close and in front of the dog. Be sure to use treats to help the dog focus on sitting still and waiting until you return to him.

Little by little, you can use fewer treats and begin to stand further away from the dog so that by the sixth week, the dog will sit and stay with you standing in front of him for a full minute. Reserve a nice tasty treat and lots of praise for when you return to him.

Solving the problem of dogs' running away or not waiting at open doorways is a major step in developing a reliable, faithful canine partner. That in itself makes for a dog/owner bond that's a priceless gem.

## "WAIT"

Usually the dog can be taught to sit in a doorway and wait to be given permission to go outside. Start that "wait" training with the dog on lead and you holding the loop end of the lead as you walk through the doorway or get out of the car. Insist that the dog wait until you give the command "OK" before he can move. By the time you're ready to practice waiting in doorways, the dog should be weaned off the food rewards and just obeying for the enthusiastic praise he receives when he's finished.

# SEPARATION ANXIETY

*The dog waited for hours for his owner to return. At first he paced the house, smelling things that carried the scent of his leader. He curled up on the boss's chair and waited. He went to the window a dozen times. He wandered the house trying to find a secure place to rest, a place that smelled like his owner.*

*Finally he settled on the sofa. As he rested there, he felt the need to chew on something, so he started sniffing the fabric of the sofa. He caught the owner's scent on the arm of the sofa and he began to lick it. Next, he nibbled the fabric. Finally he began to chew the material. The more he chewed, the more frustrated he became until he turned to digging at the sofa cushion.*

*By the time the owner returned home at the end of the day, the sofa stuffing was scattered all over the living room and the sofa looked like a complete shambles. It was no longer recognizable as a sofa, just a mass of stuffing and shredded fabric.*

Whether it's called separation anxiety, separation frustration, alone syndrome or anything else, the problem is the same. Being a social animal, the dog needs a pack and a pack leader in order to feel secure and function appropriately in life. When he's separated from his pack, he experiences feelings of anxiety and apprehension. In some dogs, this feeling of fear and worry is so strong that he attempts to relieve the feeling by a wide variety of behaviors.

Behaviors like excessive barking, howling, digging at the floor, walls or furniture, urinating or defecating and chewing on anything he can get his mouth around (even his own body parts, such as his feet) are all ways in which the dog tries to cope with the fear and anxiety of being alone. Unfortunately, they are all behaviors that owners find unacceptable.

Some owners see these behaviors as acts of spite because the dog was left alone. This is untrue; dogs do not experience the emotion of spitefulness. Therefore, by understanding the cause of the dog's destructive behavior when he's left alone, we can prevent problems of this nature. In other words, to correct

Some dogs spend the day keeping a constant watch, awaiting the return of their beloved owners.

any of the various behavior problems associated with separation anxiety, we must first understand how the dog feels about being separated from his pack before we can change his negative behavior.

As we've learned, dogs, like humans, are social animals. Leadership is a social function designed to help maintain peaceful unity within a group of individuals. That's a fancy way of saying that in order for a group to live together in harmony, the group must have a leader. Furthermore, in order to survive, all members must honor the leader. With dogs and humans the rules of the pack serve to strengthen the bond between dog and owner. In short, the dog wants to please his leader.

## A PLACE OF HIS OWN

Dogs are social creatures and do not fare well when isolated from their packs. Anxiety in these situations is usually manifested in such behaviors as destructive chewing, barking, digging, excessive panting, hyperventilating, inappropriate urinating and defecating and fence jumping. If the owner cannot be there to supervise him, the dog should be crated. This will give the dog a feeling of security when he's in his own little den or cubby. The crate should always be located in the heart of the home, where the dog is allowed to feel a part of family life. Never keep a dog in a crate in a garage, basement, laundry room or some isolated area where he cannot see, hear and smell his pack members. The importance of crate training for this and other reasons is emphasized throughout this book.

If you've allocated a certain room in which your dog can stay uncrated while you're out, he certainly will appreciate a comfy bed to cuddle up in.

A dog who feels comfortable when alone is less likely to suffer from separation anxiety. An appropriately sized crate, used properly and made cozy with soft bedding, acts as your dog's safe retreat when you're not there.

# SEPARATION ANXIETY OR BOREDOM?

If you have a dog with destructive habits and you're not sure whether the problem is caused by separation anxiety or boredom, the following quiz may help you. After each question, there are two possible answers: "a" and "b." Check the answer that relates to your dog. Then, when the quiz is completed, see the evaluations of your answers at the end.

1. Does your dog tend to chew the same thing or a whole variety of things?
   a.  The same thing
   b.  A variety of things

2. What type of things is he more likely to chew if given the opportunity?
   a.  Carpets, furniture, plants, etc.
   b.  Personal items such as clothing, shoes, handbags, etc.

3. If he chews personal items, do they belong to one particular person?
   a.  No
   b.  Yes

4. If he chews non-personal items, it the destruction centered around exits such as doors and windows?
   a.  No
   b.  Yes

5. Does he chew only when he has no access to you or sometimes when you are present as well?
   a.  Sometimes when present
   b.  Only when no access

6. Is your dog happy to be isolated from you in any room with the door closed?
   a.  Yes
   b.  No

7. If the destruction is sometimes or always accompanied by defecation and/or urination, is there just one spot to clean up or are there many?
   a.  One
   b.  Many

8. Would your dog be likely to chew when left for:
   a.  More than half an hour
   b.  Less than half an hour

9. Is he always destructive when left alone?
   a.  No
   b.  Yes

10. When you return to him, does your dog:
   a.  Avoid you
   b.  Greet you

11. If your dog greets you after something has been destroyed is he:
   a.  Excited and happy to see you
   b.  Stressed, anxious, overattached for some time after

If you checked more "b" answers, chances are the dog is suffering from separation anxiety. More "a" answers indicate that the dog is suffering from boredom.

Destructive behavior due to separation anxiety can also be caused by several other symptoms related to the dog's being isolated from his owner. Insecurity and a lack of self-confidence also contribute to the dog's fears, as does worry caused by storms and unexpected events such as strangers knocking on the door.

Boredom can be a major factor, especially in dogs that are normally active individuals. These dogs need things to do, such as working, hunting, obedience training, agility and other activities involving their owners. The destructive behaviors of these individuals are always focused on owner-scented articles. In addition, the behavior usually commences shortly after the owner leaves. It continues until either the dog's frustration is satiated or he is physically exhausted. (Tearing apart a lounge chair is hard work!)

In either case, being left alone and unsupervised is the root cause for the dog's destructive behavior. Not only do dogs not like being left alone, they do not like being left alone in large spaces. Your home, for example, is probably considered a large space by the dog.

To help dog owners understand how their dogs are feeling, I often tell my students that being left alone in the house to a dog is like your being left

## BORN TO CHEW
Certain breeds of dog are more likely to develop particular destructive behaviors than others. Certain breeds are more natural chewers than other breeds. Before acquiring a dog, people should research their breed of choice to determine the likelihood of the dog's being a chewer. For this and many other reasons, it behooves a dog buyer to gather as much information about a particular breed before purchasing a dog. However, any individual can turn out to be a chewer.

## DEN IN THE WILD

If you think about a dog or a wolf in the wild, the animal always seeks a small place just big enough for him to curl up in and sleep. This may be a spot like a hole dug into the side of a riverbank, or a small space under the roots of a big tree. Your own dog may often seek a resting place under a large table or behind a chair or sofa or, when outdoors, may snoop around to find an out-of-the-way spot in the yard. The den instincts explain why a cozy spot like a crate gives the dog a sense of security.

comfortable. Instead, you'd begin to look for a small cozy space where you could wait until dawn, and you probably would not sleep much that night, either!

The solution to separation anxiety, then, is giving the dog a small cozy space in which to wait for you where he will not feel fearful or lonely. A dog crate is most often the answer. Either a wire crate or a fiberglass airline-type carrier can be made suitable, providing that it's big enough so the dog can lie down and rest comfortably and stand up without having his head hit the top of the crate. Providing a crate that's too large will not give the dog the security of a space that's just big enough for him.

Separation anxiety can be avoided by providing a small, secure, comfortable place for the dog to stay while he's alone, and being safe in his crate protects your home, your furnishings and your dog from harm. When you return, you and the dog can celebrate being together again without the unpleasantness of contending with the results of destructive behavior.

One additional note here: for the dog suffering from boredom, it isn't enough just to return home to be with the dog. He will need mental and physical stimulation; this is essential throughout the dog's entire life. He's an active dog and he needs to do things

alone in a sports stadium and being told that you must spend the night there by yourself. What a frightening thought! You certainly wouldn't feel secure and

whenever possible. Keeping him busy and providing a crate for him to use when you can't be with him are both essential ingredients in good management of your dog.

The steps for successfully crate-training a dog are spelled out in the chapter on house-training. Remember to complete each and every step, in the order in which they are listed. Soon

**CLEAN CRATE TIP**

Never put food or water in the crate with the dog. When he ingests food or water, his digestive system begins working and sooner or later he will need to relieve himself. If he's in his crate and you're not home when that happens, he will be forced to soil his crate. Dogs do not like to stay in soiled areas, so that will create house-training problem for you and the dog.

Dogs need constructive ways to occupy themselves when their owners are out or busy, so that they don't spend all of their time just waiting by the door.

A fenced yard is a wonderful place to give your dogs time for free running and exercise, but they should never be left out there all day. Most breeds thrive as members of the family and need to be part of life in the home.

you will have a dog who loves his crate and the security it represents. Often a dog will choose to rest in his crate even when his owner is home because he feels so comfortable there.

This is a sign that the dog truly loves his special space. This method has proved successful for thousands of dogs and their owners. Now let it work for you and your dog.

"Is it time to go outside yet?" Owners who are away for most of the day must make extra efforts to include their dogs in evening and weekend activities.

Peeking out from behind the security of the fence to see what's going on.

# SHYNESS

Shyness can be genetic in nature or caused by something that has happened in the dog's environment to make him avoid people, animals, places or activities. Sometimes he expresses shyness toward a combination of causes, such as a particular place and a particular person. For example, a dog that is abused by his owner when the dog is out in the yard may exhibit shyness whenever he's in the yard and the owner appears. At other times, when the dog is in the yard and the owner is not present, he may be fine and unafraid.

For the genetically shy dog, a carefully planned program of rehabilitation may help him to

**SUPERVISION REQUIRED**

Rehabilitating a genetically shy dog should be done under the supervision and assistance of an experienced professional dog behaviorist. Without such a person's guidance, simple errors in training can result in permanent damage to the dog's psyche. Most veterinarians can refer clients to qualified dog behaviorists for shyness treatment.

get control of his shyness, although he will never be completely free of it. Genes play a very strong role in determining behavior. They influence much of an animal's behavior from birth to death.

The dog that is shy due to heredity is often shy of most unfamiliar places, people and activities throughout his life. He lacks self-confidence and the ability to cope with a variety of situations in his everyday surroundings. However, he can be helped by exposure to confidence-building activities and owners who are willing and able to devote

A puppy may be shy during the first few days in his new home, but once he starts to feel comfortable, his true personality will shine through.

the time to habituate the dog to a near-normal lifestyle.

It must be understood that, once successful at habituation, the dog will always exhibit shyness toward anything and everything that is new and unfamiliar to him. Therefore, whenever the dog is exposed to new things, the owner must help the dog become habituated to each new thing before the dog will accept it as part of his normal environment.

As for the dog that exhibits non-genetic shyness, a training program to help the dog overcome the problem may be instituted by the owner. Once again, before we can help the

dog, we must determine the cause of his shyness to a particular situation or individual. Let's look at some common causes for non-genetic shyness. Most of these causes can be cured by patience, understanding and a simple program of rehabilitation implemented by the owner.

Kennelosis is a non-genetic condition created when a puppy is not socialized at an early age. He is kept in the kennel or breeder's home and not given opportunities to meet other people and dogs or experience a variety of places and activities. That is why kindergarten puppy classes are so good for puppies.

Bringing your dog along with you as often as possible is a wonderful way to socialize him. Soon you'll have a "dog about town" who's eager to meet the world.

You can tell a lot about a puppy's personality by doing a few simple tests, such as handling him, looking for eye contact and seeing how readily he approaches you.

They meet many other puppies and people (both adults and children), they are exposed to a wide variety of fun and interesting experiences and they learn basic manners while discovering that learning itself is fun.

The most common cases of kennelosis come when a breeder keeps a puppy as a prospective show dog. The breeder is busy and does not socialize the puppy while waiting to see how the puppy will develop by the time he is five or six months old. When the breeder finally decides that the puppy does not measure up to show standards, the breeder offers the pup for sale as a pet.

A person purchases the now six-month-old puppy and takes the dog to his home. In the new, strange environment, the puppy becomes so stressed at being removed from the only home he's ever known that he can't function normally. He expresses his fear of the unknown in many ways. He shivers constantly, he hides in dark corners, he doesn't eat, he's unable to make friends with family members and he frequently urinates submissively. In other words, he acts so shy that life for him is traumatic and he's obviously miserable.

The new owner eventually takes the puppy back to the breeder. Chances are, he will live out his life in the safety and comfort of his birth home, where he feels secure. This sad scenario can be found in any breed of dog, including mixed breeds. If the puppy is not socialized between 8 and 16 weeks of age, in all probability he will suffer irreparable damage to his personality. Only occasionally can a long, careful program of rehabilitation help the dog overcome his lack of confidence to a point where he can assume a normal life. Some breeds seem to suffer more than others when it comes to kennelosis, so if you're contemplating purchasing a puppy suffering from this condition, talk to your veterinarian or dog behaviorist before you make your final decision.

Another often-seen reason for shyness is caused by accidental happenings. For example, a young puppy is playing in the kitchen when his owner enters the room carrying a folded-up umbrella. The puppy has never seen an umbrella. He goes over to investigate this new object.

Without thinking, the owner, who isn't paying any attention to the puppy, opens the umbrella to inspect it. As it snaps open, it makes a strange and unfamiliar noise and startles the puppy. The puppy jumps away and the owner then tries to encourage the dog to come over and investigate the object. The puppy, however, decides he doesn't want anything to do with it and he shies away

Some dogs are clingier than others, preferring to stay close to their owners.

from it. Frustrated, the owner then drags the puppy over to smell the umbrella and tells him that he's a good boy as he forces the issue on the little dog. Forcing the dog to get close to the umbrella only serves to heighten his fear.

However, slowly exposing him to the object and letting him investigate it on his own terms, while you offer support with soft words of praise for being so brave, can eventually help the dog overcome his fear of the umbrella. This method of slow and careful exposure to a feared object over an extended period of time usually works very well. We simply make the feared object a regular part of the dog's environment so that he no longer concerns himself with it and accepts it as normal. By manipulating the environment, we can change the dog's behavior.

Some dogs are afraid of people wearing hats, particularly men.

## BIG, BAD BABIES

It isn't at all unusual for a dog living in an all-adult family to be afraid of babies and little children. After all, they smell funny, they squeal and holler, they run fast and they flail their arms around in erratic patterns. What's worse, whenever they see the dog, they grab at him and pull his fur, poke at his nose and eyes and tug on his tail! In other words, they're totally unpredictable and, in the dog's perception, definitely dangerous!

Many dogs are afraid of vacuum cleaners. Others are afraid of going up and down stairs, while some are startled by and shy away from strange objects in the dark. For example, dog and owner go for a late-night walk and they come upon a trash can that is not normally there. First, the dog stops and growls at the strange figure. Then he crouches down as if he's going to attack it. Next, he stands up tall and alert, as if preparing for this "enemy" to attack him. Here again, the owner can encourage the dog to investi-

Food and happy thoughts go hand-in-hand for a dog, which is why treats are successful in coaxing a shy pup to come out of his shell around new people.

### UP AND DOWN THE STAIRS

Teaching your dog not to fear stairs uses a method called chaining. Instead of trying to get the dog to go up the stairs from the bottom, carry him to the first step from the top. Put him down and encourage him to jump up one step to the top. When he does, praise and offer a food treat. Next, carry him to the second step from the top and repeat the process. Soon he'll run up the stairs from the bottom to the top in anticipation of your praise and an occasional food reward.

gate the strange object while demonstrating to him that it is harmless. Once the dog figures out that it's an inanimate object, the owner should praise the dog for accepting the trash can as something to be ignored. We'll discuss the specifics of this training in more detail later in the chapter.

If you can imagine how the dog must feel in any of these situations, it becomes easier to understand that we must help the dog overcome his shyness while building his self-confidence. Once you can see life from your dog's point of view, you'll find it easy to help him cope with life's various experiences.

As discussed in the case of the dog afraid of umbrellas, most of these types of problems can be erased by slowly exposing the dog to the fear-causing factor. Let the dog acclimate himself to the strange object or situation while you act as his much-needed support system while he's building self-confidence.

If people wearing hats are making your dog afraid, let family members wear hats and get the dog so accustomed to seeing people wearing hats that he doesn't even think about it. Leave some hats in low places around the house where the dog can investigate and sniff them. When you see he's becoming curious about them, pick one up, put it on and take it off, and then praise the dog for being so curious and brave. Next, put it back where it was and act very casual as you resume your previous activity. Remember, if you don't act startled or fearful, the dog will be a lot less likely to be worried, too.

Sometimes dogs are afraid of the vacuum cleaner. In this case,

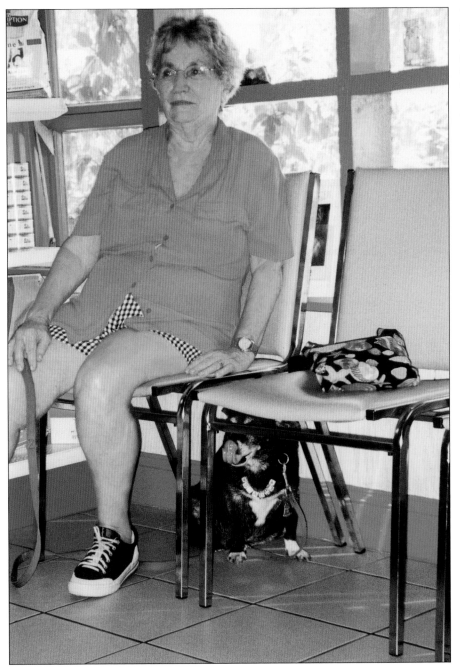

The vet's office is rarely a dog's favorite place to go, but this dog suffers from extreme shyness in unfamiliar environments and is hiding as far under his owner's chair as he can.

bring your vacuum cleaner out of the closet and set it in the middle of the room for a few days. The dog will become accustomed to seeing it there all the time. Next, turn it on and just let it run for a few minutes while you go about your normal activities. You can also take a food treat and go sit down near the vacuum cleaner as you offer the treat to the dog. Suddenly the vacuum becomes part of the scene and, when it's running, the dog gets a special treat, so he starts to like the sound of the motor rather than fear it.

To teach the dog to go down the stairs, begin by placing him on the last step before the bottom. He'll simply jump down to the floor and you can praise and reward with a treat. Next, place him on the second-to-last step and repeat the process. Again, he'll soon be going all the way down the stairs without your having to help him. Be sure to praise the dog as he builds confidence in his ability to negotiate stairs.

To acclimate a dog to strange objects in the dark, simply place objects in places where he normally doesn't see them. Expose him to them after dark and allow him to investigate them as you act as his support team. Things like bicycles, trash cans and cardboard boxes all create strange, dark images at night. You want the dog to be curious about these things,

Shyness and fear can cause some dogs to act out defensively, so muzzling a dog in fear-trigger situations, such as getting a shot, is helpful in controlling his reactions.

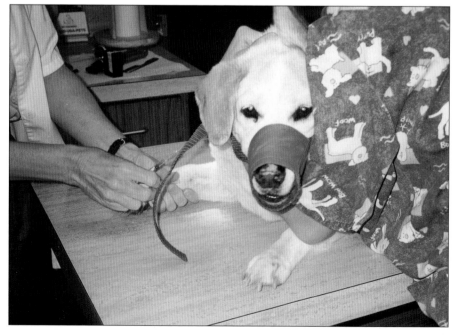

Under the chair doesn't always mean a hiding place! It could just serve as a cool shady spot on a sunny day.

but not afraid of them, so building his confidence will help him cope with his environment.

Fear of children and babies will take longer to change than fear of objects. However, it can be done with patience and understanding on your part. First, you must enlist the help of friends who have a child. Have the little one sit still and quietly on the floor. You and the dog should approach the child while the child holds a biscuit in his open palm in front of him.

Show the biscuit to the dog and encourage him to take it from the child. The child should not move, but should say "Good boy" once the dog accepts the food. As the dog becomes accustomed to taking food from the child, have the child stand. Be sure to remind the child to stand still and praise the dog when he takes the biscuit.

Little by little, you can have the dog come and sit in front of the standing child as he holds the treat for the dog. Let the child extend his hand to allow the dog to sniff it before he takes the treat. Once the dog sees that the child is not going to threaten him, you can begin to teach the child how to pet the dog under the chin and along the side of the head. Do not allow the child to raise his hand above the dog's head, as the dog may see this as an aggressive move.

Over a period of time, the child can be trained to act calmly and to use a softer voice around the dog while the animal becomes accustomed to having the child touch him and give him treats. Making the meetings short, pleasant, non-stressful and rewarding will eventually teach the dog to like children.

Acclimating dogs to babies can begin with holding a doll in your arms and encouraging the dog to investigate it as he watches you talk to it and cuddle it. Next, place the doll on a bed and tell the dog what a good boy he is while he looks but doesn't touch. When the opportunity presents itself, hold a real baby in your arms and let the dog satisfy his curiosity about this strange new "object." With the right encouragement from you, the dog will accept the baby without trying to grab, bite or even be afraid of it.

In summary, correcting the problem of shyness in a dog involves desensitizing the dog to the fear factor by gradually exposing him to the cause. As you're doing that, you replace the undesirable behavior with positive activities such as receiving food treats, playing with special toys and happy interaction with the owner. Soon the dog begins to replace the fear factor with pleasant things until his fear evaporates.

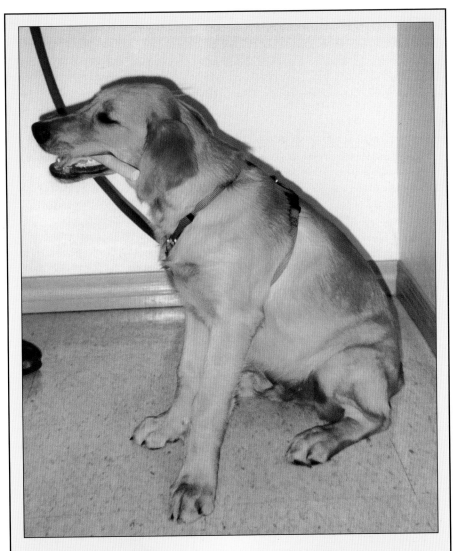

## SECURITY BLANKET

Interestingly, putting a collar and lead on the dog acts as a security measure to the dog. It's similar to a small child who carries around a ragged blanket whenever he feels stressed. When the mother attempts to remove the blanket from the child, she discovers how upset the child becomes at losing his article of security. Giving the blanket back produces the security that the child needs in order to cope with whatever he finds stressful. The collar and lead do the same thing for the dog.

# STEALING FOOD

## "LEAVE IT"

Some dogs will learn this lesson quickly while others, particularly the stubborn ones, will take many hours of practice for success. The command "Leave it!" means that you want the dog to stop doing whatever he's doing immediately. All dogs should be taught the "Leave it" command from an early age. When the dog accepts your command and settles down near the plate of food without reaching for it, reward the dog with a biscuit of his own. Soon he'll learn that your food belongs to you and his biscuits belong to him when he obeys your commands.

Many dogs will steal food when they can get to it and if their owners are not present. Still bolder individuals will attempt to steal food in the presence of their owners. Regardless, stealing food at any time and under any circumstances is a very undesirable behavior. In fact, there have been occasions when dogs have stolen food that almost killed them!

I recall a lovely black Labrador who stole and ate a whole box of chocolate Easter candy. By the time the owner discovered it, the dog was violently ill and had to be rushed to the veterinarian right away, as chocolate is toxic to dogs. The doctor managed to save the dog, but the Lab was a mighty sick pup for almost a week before he recovered.

The most obvious solution to preventing a dog from stealing food when you are not present is to never leave food out where the dog can get to it. Even food wrapped in aluminum or plastic wrap is not safe around a dog if he's determined to get it.

You can set up a situation in which you put out some food and leave the room but hide nearby where you can observe the dog to see if he attempts to get at the food. When he takes scent of the food and goes to investigate it, you can throw something near the dog to startle him and make him turn away from the food source. A small can into which you have placed some little stones or coins that will make a loud rattling sound is ideal for this. Close the can's opening with some electrical tape. Be sure, however, not to hit

Playing begging games at the table encourages food-stealing behaviors. Here's my editor Andrew DePrisco with his naughty but lovely Shiba, Kabuki.

To prevent begging and food-stealing tendencies, teach your dogs to act politely around food, such as waiting for their food bowls.

the dog with the can. Just have the can land near enough to him to startle him.

As soon as he turns away, you will rush into the room and praise him for leaving the food alone. Reward him with one of his own biscuits and lots of praise. Do not let the dog see you with the can at any time or he'll associate you with the scary noisemaker. This prearranged scenario works well with some, but not with all, dogs.

If a dog develops a habit of stealing food when you are present, you must first ask yourself how the

A plastic baggie is no match for a dog's sense of smell. Add to that the fact that he can see the food, and he's going to try to get it.

Motivated by an interesting smell and the potential to find a morsel to eat, dogs may display behavior that's less than polite by human standards.

Practicing on leash, the dog is being trained to wait for his owner's "OK" to go to his food bowl.

## THAT'S WILD!

It is important to keep in mind that stealing food, like so many other undesirable behaviors, is a carry-over from the dog's wild days. It simply stayed with him into domestication. (Chasing is another carry-over behavior from the days when the dog had to chase and catch his prey in order to survive.)

habit began. Chances are he reached up and helped himself to some food on a plate while you watched, perhaps in disbelief, but didn't react quickly enough to stop him. He then learned that helping himself to your food was fine. Thus a new behavior was formed.

To retrain a dog to leave forbidden food alone, put his collar and lead on the dog. Set a plate of food on a table and approach the table with the dog. Let the dog take scent of the food and immediately have him sit and stay. Be firm about this and don't let the dog keep popping up to get at the food. An authoritative command of "Stay, leave it!" combined with a short lead to keep tight control of the dog will, sooner or later, have the dog accepting the fact that you're the boss and you will not accept anything but compliance.

Feeding your dog twice a day instead of once often helps curb some of his urge to steal food. Control the dog so he doesn't have opportunities to steal your food. Don't leave food unattended when you're not around. These are all things you can do to lessen the dog's urge to steal. If the urge disappears, it will be easier to keep the dog busy with acceptable activities and out of trouble.

Successful steal! Be careful, though, because food stealing is not discouraged for behavior reasons only; sweets and other kinds of "people food" are not good for dogs, and some are even toxic.

# INDEX

Activity 59, 91, 104
Aggression
—dealing with 22
—fearful 14
—maternal 14
—predatory 14
—reason for 13
—sexual 14
—territorial 14
—toward animals 18
—toward children 16
Alerting barking 24
Anxiety 98, 102
Attention-getting barking 28
Barking 24, 98
—causes of 24
—nuisance 74
Bedding 67
"Bicky" 94
Bones 58
Boredom 31, 102-104
—digging 57
Cars 34
—chasing 40
—safety 37
—sickness 34
Chaining 114
Chase instinct 39, 124
Chasing
—cats 18
—children 39
—games 75
—syndrome 40
—vehicles 40
Chewing 98, 103
—causes of 43
Children 15, 16-18, 39, 80, 95, 118
Chocolate 120
Clutter method 88
Come 93, 96
Commands 68, 71, 93, 96-97
Communication barking 29, 32

Confidence 103, 109
Consistency 69
Control 67, 69
Controlled jumping 90
Coprophagia 55
Crate 65, 100, 104
—training 59, 64, 105
—types of 66
Danger 76, 92
Denning instinct 104
Desensitization training 61
Destructive behavior 50, 98, 100, 103
—determining causes of 102
Digging 56, 98
—causes of 57
Dog/owner bond 32, 97
Domestication 124
Dominance 11, 22
Eating stool 55
Escaping 89, 92
Excitement barking 32
Exercise 59
Fear 60, 98, 103, 109
—barking 26
—biting 13, 23
—of objects 112-116
Fearful aggression 14
Feeding 125
Fenced yard 89, 92
Food
—jumping up for 84
—rewards 81, 93
—stealing 120
Forbidden items 76
Frustration 32
—as a cause of digging 57
Furniture 86
Genetic shyness 109
Hormonal jumping 84
Hormones 64
Hot weather 43, 57
House-training 45, 64, 105
—elements of 69
—schedule 66
—steps 68

Howling 98
Insecurity 103
Investigative jumping 84
Isolation frustration 46, 91, 98, 100, 103
Jumping
—causes of 78
—controlled 90
—due to hormones 84
—for his food 84
—on command 90
—on furniture 86
—on people 78, 80-81
—over fences 89
—to investigate 84
Keeping cool 57
Kennelosis 110-112
Kindergarten puppy classes 110
Leadership 98, 100
Leave it 71, 120, 125
Marking territory 64, 69
Maternal aggression 14
Motion sickness 34
Mounting 86
Mousetrap method 87
Neurotic behavior 57
Neutering 64, 86
Noises 60
Non-genetic shyness 110
Nuisance barking 74
"Only dog" 21
Other animals 18
Pack animal 98, 100
Play behavior 73
Positive reinforcement 33, 81, 93
Pots and pans method 88
Praise 67-69, 123
Predatory aggression 14
Punishment 56
Retrieving a buried object 57
Reward 81, 123
Rough play 73

Running away 92
Safety 18, 37, 76, 104, 120
Schedule for house-training 66
Security 119
Separation anxiety 59, 98
Sexual aggression 14
Shyness 109
Sit 80-81
Social animals 46, 98, 100
Socialization 109
Spaying 64, 86
Stair climbing 114
Stay 96, 125
Stealing food 120
Stool eating 55
Storms 60
Strangers 14-18, 25-26
Submissiveness 11
Supervision 69
Survival instinct 124
Teething 43
Tension 58
Territorial aggression 14
Thunder 60
Topical aggression 13
Toys 58, 77
Training 93, 97
Traveling
—safety 37
—sickness 34
Treats 37, 81, 93-94
Tug-of-war games
—inadvisability of 73
Types of aggression 14
Urinating 98
Urine marking 64, 69
Vehicle chasing 40-41
Veterinarian 86
Wait. 34, 97
Water pistol, use of 41
"Where are you?" game 94

# Kennel Club Books™

The pet-book authority, Kennel Club Books
is currently producing the

## WORLD'S LARGEST SERIES OF DOG-BREED BOOKS,

including individual titles on 377 different dog
breeds, representing every American Kennel Club
recognized breed as well as hundreds of other rare
breeds for which no title currently exists in English.

Each Kennel Club Breed Book is at least 158
pages, completely illustrated in color, with a
hard-bound cover. The prestigious roster of
authors includes world authorities in their
breeds, as well as famous breeders,
veterinarians, artists and trainers.

Explore the world of dogs by visiting
kennelclubbooks.com on the Web and find
out more about available titles on fascinating
pure-bred dogs from around the globe.

## Kennel Club Books, LLC
308 Main Street, Allenhurst, NJ 07711 USA
(732) 531-1995 • www.kennelclubbooks.com